250-93

D0305755

Columbia University

Contributions to Education

Teachers College Series

No. 627

AMS PRESS
NEW YORK

Inter-Institutional Agreements
in Higher Education

146245

AN ANALYSIS OF THE DOCUMENTS
RELATING TO INTER-INSTITUTIONAL AGREEMENTS
WITH SPECIAL REFERENCE TO COORDINATION

BY

DANIEL SAMMIS SANFORD, Jr., Ph.D.

Teachers College, Columbia University
Contributions to Education, No. 627

Published with the Approval of
Professor F. B. O'Rear, *Sponsor*

LB2341
S25
1972

BUREAU OF PUBLICATIONS
TEACHERS COLLEGE, COLUMBIA UNIVERSITY
NEW YORK CITY
1934

Library of Congress Cataloging in Publication Data

Sanford, Daniel Sammis, 1902-
    Inter-institutional agreements in higher education.

    Reprint of the 1934 ed., issued in series:
Teachers College, Columbia University. Contributions
to education, no. 627.
    Originally presented as the author's thesis,
Columbia.
    Includes bibliographical references.
    1. Universities and colleges--United States--
Administration. 2. Intellectual cooperation.
I. Title. II. Series: Columbia University.
Teachers College. Contributions to education,
no. 627.
LB2341.S25 1972   378.1'04   75-177226
ISBN 0-404-55627-2

Reprinted by Special Arrangement with Teachers
College Press, New York, New York

From the edition of 1934, New York
First AMS edition published in 1972
Manufactured in the United States

AMS PRESS, INC.
NEW YORK, N. Y.   10003

9.85

PREFACE

THOSE acquainted with inter-institutional agreements in higher education throughout the country recognize the need for an inclusive study of this instrument of coordination. Too often agreements have been worked out with little knowledge of the structure and function of cooperative arrangements developed elsewhere. The present study represents an initial attempt to examine all agreements known to be in operation between higher educational institutions. The belief is held that more extensive knowledge than heretofore available of this instrument is appropriate at the present time when there is widespread demand on higher educational institutions for greater adaptation. Such knowledge, it is believed, may prove of value to institutions contemplating agreements, participating in agreements, or in situations where agreements may be possible. Of necessity, the present study has been limited to an investigation of the documents setting forth the terms of agreements and to other descriptive materials. It is hoped that in future other studies will be made of agreements as they function in operation and as they are employed for accomplishing institutional and social objectives.

The author wishes to express his indebtedness to the members of his committee for their interest and cooperation in the present study. He is especially indebted to Professor F. B. O'Rear, who kindly acted as sponsor for the investigation and whose valuable counsel at various points was of very great assistance. Professor John L. Childs, Professor M. C. Del Manzo, Provost of Teachers College, and Professor Donald G. Tewksbury, acting as advisers for the study, gave generously of their time and advice. He also wishes to express appreciation to Professor Donald P. Cottrell, Professor Clarence Linton, Secretary of Teachers College, and Professor E. S. Evenden, who read the entire manuscript and made valuable suggestions. Finally, appreciation is due to the large number of persons representing various colleges and universities, who kindly furnished copies of the documents of agreements for this study and who gave their assistance in making available additional information.

D. S. S., Jr.

CONTENTS

CHAPTER   PAGE

I. THE TREND TOWARD COORDINATION   I
    Larger Groupings among Higher Educational Institutions . . .   2
    Changes in Higher Education Fostering Coordination   7

II. DEFINITION AND SCOPE OF STUDY   11
    Definitions   11
    Statement of the Problem   13
    Procedure   15
    Sources   15

III. EXTENT TO WHICH AGREEMENTS HAVE BEEN DEVELOPED   17
    Number of Agreements in Force   17
    Methods of Reporting Agreements   20
    Number of Agreements Formed by a Single Institution   21
    Types of Higher Institution Participating in Agreements . . .   23
    Geographical Location of Institutions Consummating Agreements   25
    Enrollment of Colleges and Universities Participating in Agree-
       ments   26
    Abrogated Agreements   26
    Agreements Not Yet Consummated   28
    Summary   28

IV. CONDITIONS GOVERNING THE FORMATION OF AGREEMENTS . . .   30
    Programs of Participating Institutions   30
    Type of Higher Institution   32
    Size of Higher Institutions   36
    Proximity of Higher Institutions   40
    Geographical and Urban Location   41
    Transportation Facilities   43
    Prospect of Financial Saving   44
    Prospect of Greater Institutional Recognition   44
    Prospect of Greater Service to the Area   45
    Summary   45

V. CHANGES IN STRUCTURE AND FUNCTION RESULTING FROM AGREE-
    MENT   47
    Control   47
    Administration   52
    Faculty   56
    Facilities   61
    Summary   70

Contents

CHAPTER   PAGE
VI. INSTITUTIONAL IDENTITY AND POWERS UNDER AGREEMENT . . .   71
  Integrity of Charters   71
  Identity and General Powers of Corporations   72
  Control of Property and Finance   72
  Control of Program   73
  Control of Students   74
  Powers for Modification and Termination of Agreements   74
  Summary   77

VII. VALUES SOUGHT UNDER AGREEMENT   78
  Enlarged and Increased Offerings without Loss to Institutional
    Programs   78
  Decreased Institutional Expense with the Same or Increased
    Service   80
  Preservation and Increase in Standards of Achievement   82
  The Same or Increased Recognition for Allied Institutions . . .   83
  Preservation and Augmentation of Institutional Distinctive Char-
    acter   84
  Preservation of Identity and Powers under Agreement   87
  Cooperative Planning of Higher Education for an Area   87
  Possible Loss of Values   88

VIII. SOME CHARACTERISTICS OF UNDESIRABLE AGREEMENTS   91
  From the Standpoint of Society   91
  From the Standpoint of Higher Educational Institutions . . .   92

IX. COOPERATIVE PLANNING IN HIGHER EDUCATION   94
  Summary   109

X. GENERAL SUMMARY AND CONCLUSIONS   110

TABLES

TABLE   PAGE

I. Inter-institutional Agreements in Operation Among Higher Educational Institutions   18

II. Method of Reporting 115 Agreements Entered into by Higher Educational Institutions   21

III. Practice of Higher Educational Institutions of Participating in More Than One Agreement   22

IV. Types of Higher Educational Institution Participating in 115 Inter-institutional Agreements   23

V. Types of Privately Supported Higher Educational Institution Participating in Agreements with Public Institutions   24

VI. Number of Inter-institutional Agreements Found in Nine Geographical Divisions of the United States   25

VII. Enrollment for 55 Colleges and Universities Participating in Inter-institutional Agreements and Number of Agreements Formed   37

VIII. Percentage of Agreements Formed by Colleges and Universities of Different Enrollments   38

IX. Density of Population in Nine Geographical Divisions of the United States and the Number of Agreements Formed   41

X. Number of Agreements Participated in by Higher Institutions in 10 Biggest Cities of the United States   42

vii

Inter-Institutional Agreements
in Higher Education

CHAPTER I

The Trend toward Coordination

APPARENT in almost all activities is a trend toward the formation of larger and larger groupings. Widespread separate and competitive development, in the opinion of many writers on the subject, has definitely passed. Instead there is occurring with utmost certainty a movement toward integration and coordination.

This movement is most pronounced in the field of industry. There integration has gained strength until much of the industry of the nation is at present concentrated in the hands of great quasi-public corporations. Industry in certain fields is entirely under their control. Recent investigators have pointed out, moreover, that there is every probability that the trend in future will be carried further, with industry controlled in units of increasing size.[1] They say that no limit can be predicted for this tendency except the ability of human beings to manage great aggregations of property. Since their forecast was made the movement toward larger groupings has become even more apparent. Under the President's recovery program increasing appreciation is found of the interrelationship of all commercial enterprise and there is occurring an awakened consciousness of the need for coordination.

A similar trend is to be noted in the structure of society. Separate communities which were looked upon as independent and self-sufficient are linked together by ever closer bonds. "Large cities seldom appear isolated. They are almost always surrounded by a cluster of smaller centers, varying in size, which are economically and socially intertwined."[2] The trend, without doubt, is toward coordination of activities.

The metropolitan community, it is reported, is taking on "more and more the aspects of a coherent economic and cultural state, more

[1] Berle, Adolph A. and Means Gardiner C., *Modern Corporation and Private Property*, p. 18. Commerce Clearing House, Inc., New York, 1932.

[2] Report of the President's Research Committee on Recent Social Trends, *Recent Social Trends in the United States*. McKenzie, R. D., "The Rise of the Metropolitan Community," Vol. I, p. 448. McGraw-Hill Book Co. New York, 1933.

I

realistic in many ways than the existing political states."[3] With the passing of traditional divisions and with greater concentration of population within the local area, there is found an extension of the field within which local activities are carried on in common. There is occurring greater mobility of people and products, wider range of individual choice, greater specialization of local services, and more closely knit community structure.[4] These changes have resulted in the consolidation of churches and synods, the establishment of centers of medicine, the organization of branch libraries, community chest campaigns, and the formation of regional and community associations. At the same time there has occurred differentiation of services among local agencies in the attempt to do away with duplication. People now go longer distances for the services they seek, and an institution is increasingly effective in the degree that it makes a contribution to the entire area. An institution's contribution depends upon its ability to develop service of high quality and this in large measure depends upon its ability to specialize its activities.

The modification of social structure has led very naturally to attempts at social planning. Both present and future needs have compelled interest in controlled development. In addition to traffic and highway planning, provision is being made for parks and districts are being zoned. An entire city, county, or region has been chosen as a field for social planning. Indication is that the immediate future will see the planning of vast areas, such as, for example, the Tennessee Valley.

LARGER GROUPINGS AMONG HIGHER EDUCATIONAL INSTITUTIONS

Like other agencies in society, higher institutions have increasingly felt the demand for coordination of their services. Attention on their part is being directed beyond the old unit of the institution to the new unit of the state or region. More and more institutions are concerned with the contribution they make to society.

Particularly has this concern developed in the case of public institutions. Serious doubts have arisen in the minds of the people of the state due to the competitive activities which have characterized the relations of state universities, colleges of agriculture and mechanic arts, teachers colleges, women's colleges, junior colleges, and normal schools. It has been seen that in the interest of greater economy and

[3] McKenzie, *op. cit.,* p. 445.
[4] *Ibid.,* p. 493.

more adequate provision duplication must be avoided and that there must be differentiation through allocation of particular endeavor to different institutions. This necessity has led to integration and coordination. In a recent report it is stated that "all told, fourteen states (Florida, Georgia, Idaho, Iowa, Kansas, Mississippi, Montana, New York, North Carolina, North Dakota, Oklahoma, Oregon, South Dakota, West Virginia) have taken steps toward partial or complete unification of their educational offerings, although in one (Oklahoma) the plan has largely been given over."[5]

Private institutions also show a tendency toward integration. In some cases they have merged, a single institution taking over the property of another or the assets of both being combined to form a new institution. In other cases larger groupings have been brought about through agreement, each institution retaining its identity and independence but at the same time entering into some form of cooperation. Coordination through both of these methods has increased the opportunities which the institutions were able to provide separately. Greater facilities have been placed at the disposal of their students and new opportunities have been developed for advanced or specialized training.

Coordination among private institutions has occurred most frequently where institutions are located in a metropolitan area. It is interesting to note that Columbia University, located in the largest city of the country, has formed the greatest number of agreements. Columbia has developed into a federated university linked to various professional schools and colleges in the New York area and also to institutions which do not provide formal education, such as museums, hospitals, and libraries. In other cities similar development has taken place. Noting this trend President Nicholas Murray Butler predicted the growth of large federated institutions in urban location where there was already established a strong university.[6] New York, Boston, Philadelphia, Chicago, and Berkeley (California) seemed to him to be the probable regions where such federated universities would arise. Since his prediction was made

[5] Kelly, Fred J. and McNeely, John H., *The State and Higher Education; Phases of Their Relationship*, p. vii. The Carnegie Foundation for the Advancement of Teaching in cooperation with the U. S. Office of Education, Department of the Interior. New York, 1933.

[6] *Papers Relative to the Proposed Incorporation of St. Stephen's College, Annandale, New York, in the Educational System of Columbia University*, p. 4. Columbia University Press, New York, 1928.

the trend in this direction has received greater emphasis. In the Philadelphia region a plan is reported for coordination of graduate instruction. On the joint committee working out this plan sit representatives of the University of Pennsylvania, Bryn Mawr, Haverford and Swarthmore Colleges, and the Franklin Institute.[7] Furthermore, a project of larger scope is reported for the Chicago region. The University of Chicago and Northwestern University are formulating a plan of cooperation whose purpose, according to the newspaper announcement, is the most effective application of their combined resources to the needs of the area.[8]

The regions specified by Dr. Butler, however, are not the only ones where federated universities are developing in urban location. A similar trend, as indicated by the list of agreements in Chapter III, is apparent in Albany, Atlanta, Cincinnati, Cleveland, Los Angeles, St. Louis, and possibly in other cities, such as Nashville, Omaha, and Pittsburgh.

Coordination is also taking place among higher institutions outside the urban region. This is occurring among both public and private institutions and in certain cases between public and private institutions. The former divisions which separated them are losing their power to hold them apart. Public institutions have entered into agreements with privately endowed universities and also with private schools of archeology, art, law, music, and pharmacy. Even the theological school and the denominational college have formed agreements with public institutions.

An outstanding example of cooperation between a public and a private institution is the plan of cooperation worked out between Wesley College, formerly Red River University, and the University of North Dakota. The principles governing this cooperation are well presented in the preamble to the agreement:

> It is recognized that the State University is a civic institution, and has for its mission the training of the youth of the state for efficient service as citizens. It is recognized also that the distinctive object of the church in

[7] Reported by Dr. Edward W. Mumford, Secretary, University of Pennsylvania.

[8] "University 'Merger' Studied in the Mid-West." *New York Times,* August 27, 1933. On February 25, 1934 in the *New York Times* another announcement appeared entitled "Universities Reject Merger at Chicago." It was stated that "the proposal of a merger of the two universities be laid aside and the committees discharged" *but* "that the presidents of the two universities continue to consider the possibilities of such closer cooperation as will produce the best results for higher education."

maintaining schools of its own is to insure trained leadership in religious and denominational work. There is, therefore, logically, no conflict between their respective missions for the same young people are to serve in both these capacities. These two missions being in no sense antagonistic, but supplementary, it would seem the part of wise economy that these two educational agencies should avail themselves, so far as possible, of the facilities and appliances of each other in the working out of their respective missions, keeping always in view the principle of the separation of the church and state in so far as regards the control and expenditure of the financial resources of each.

Accepting the foregoing principles as fundamentally sound, the University of North Dakota cordially invites the people of the various denominations of the state to the consideration of a plan under which the members of the several denominations, while preserving their denominational identity and maintaining separate institutions for such educational work as they may deem necessary, shall join, as citizens, in patronage of the State University as the common agency for higher education of the youth of the state.[9]

This plan of cooperation is similar to and undoubtedly was influenced by the practice of certain Canadian provincial universities whereby colleges of several denominations have been linked to the university through "affiliation" or "federation." The terms "affiliation" and "federation" are used loosely among Canadian institutions and have different implications from one institution to another. Affiliation "usually implies representation in the Senate of the affiliating body, participation in examination procedure, and recognition of part or all of the academic work of the affiliated institution for credit toward the degree of the central organization. It differs from 'federation' as at Toronto, in that the staffs of the affiliated institutions are bodies separate and independent from the central university."[10]

Coordination of the activities and endeavors of independent institutions makes possible the planning of higher education. Planning has occurred not only for the state but also for the area and for the city. An outstanding example is the Cleveland Conference for Educational Cooperation. The origin of the Conference was a study

[9] "Plan of Affiliation of Church College with State University. Probably the First Document of Its Kind in the History of Higher Education in the United States." University of North Dakota, 1925. The agreement between Wesley College and the University of North Dakota was adopted by vote of the Trustees of the latter on May 16, 1905.

[10] Learned, W. S. and Wallace, E. W., *Local Provision for Higher Education in Saskatchewan. An Advisory Memorandum on University Policy Proposed at the Request of the University of Saskatchewan*, p. 5. The Carnegie Foundation for the Advancement of Teaching, New York, 1932.

undertaken by Western Reserve University and the Case School of Applied Science. Four objectives of this study were formulated: ". . . the needs of Cleveland in its several fields of higher education; the extent to which Western Reserve University and the Case School of Applied Science were meeting those needs; the extent to which the present facilities of the two institutions should be supplemented by additional facilities; and finally a plan for some permanent cooperative organization between the two institutions in order to insure adequate development of higher education in the city."[11] The Conference seeks to enlist all agencies for higher education within the city of Cleveland. In it there meet representatives from professional schools, libraries, museums, Christian associations, and other agencies as well as from the University and the Case School. The Conference is described as follows:

> It is an educational clearing-house, a place where its members may confer and where the effort may be made to discover the educational and cultural needs of the community as a whole, the part which each of the associated institutions has in meeting those needs, the extent to which these institutions as a group are rendering the service called for, the amount of duplicated effort, and the opportunities that, singly or collectively, are being neglected. The Conference is unofficial, without authority, and in no way interferes with the activities or the independence of its members.[12]

This attempt to plan higher education finds its counterpart in other countries. An outstanding example is the city of London. Coordination is effected there through the University of London and provisions for coordination are set forth in the instructions given the Haldane Commission, which was appointed to report on the reconstitution of the University. The Commission's report led to the University Act of 1926. The Haldane Commission was instructed:

> . . . to inquire into the working of the organisation of the University of London, and into other facilities for advanced education (general, professional and technical) existing in London for persons of either sex above secondary school age; to consider what provisions should exist in the Metropolis for University teaching and research; to make recommendations as to the relations which in consequence should subsist between the University of London, its incorporated colleges, the Imperial College of Science and Technology, the

[11] Vinson, Robert E., "Coordination within the City," *The Journal of Higher Education*, Vol. IV, No. 3, p. 113, March 1933.

[12] *The Cleveland Conference for Educational Cooperation. Annual Report and Committee Reports, 1928*, p. 5. The Cleveland Conference for Educational Cooperation, Euclid Ave., Cleveland, Ohio, 1928.

other Schools of the University and the various public institutions and bodies concerned; and further to recommend as to any changes of constitutions and organisation which appear desirable; regard being had to the facilities for education and research which the metropolis should afford for specialists and advanced students in connection with the provisions in other parts of the United Kingdom and of our dominions beyond the seas.[18]

CHANGES IN HIGHER EDUCATION FOSTERING COORDINATION

American higher education during the past hundred years has undergone radical changes, many of which have fostered coordination of independent institutions. Traditionally the American college is a local, denominational institution which enrolls a comparatively small number of students. It was founded in practically all cases by individual initiative and was designed to serve a limited area or group from which its students came and in which its graduates would eventually settle. The independent and unrelated development of higher institutions came about as a direct result of their local character, their sectarian affiliation which prevented cooperation, pioneer conditions in which they were established, and strong loyalties of alumni and constituencies. Like the development of other enterprises in the United States, higher education has been carried on by large numbers of small institutions from one end of the country to the other. Only in the case of state universities and later land-grant colleges were these institutions looked upon as agencies to serve an extended geographical area.

With the changes which have occurred in American life the necessity for great numbers of independent institutions has diminished. Isolation has very largely passed before the influence of larger social groupings, more ample facilities for transportation and communication, and greater mobility of population. Students now attend colleges from great distances and the students of the local area often go elsewhere for the training they seek. Denominational influence, which was of such importance during the past century, is on the wane and in a great proportion of the cases has completely disappeared as a determinant of college offerings. Even the church-related institution no longer draws its students and support from a single sectarian group but frequently enrolls more students of other faiths than of its own.

These changes have forced all institutions to offer more and more

[18] *University of London, Calendar for the Year, 1929-30*, p. 29. University of London, South Kensington, S.W. 7, 1929.

similar programs of study. All institutions have become to an increasing degree public institutions, which serve the interests of society rather than of a limited area or group. In consequence, traditional divisions between higher institutions have tended to drop out, making possible cooperation and coordination of effort.

Concurrently other changes have fostered coordination. The past fifty years have witnessed an immense expansion in the fields of knowledge. New subjects have found their way into the curriculum and old subjects have broken down into new units. Society has made ever greater demands on all higher educational institutions, and these demands the single institution has found increasingly difficult to meet. Specialization in all fields has resulted in the necessity for a larger teaching force to present adequately the subject matter of a standard course. A growing popularity of higher education has brought a larger and larger proportion of the general population to the doors of the college. The diverse interests of these students have required enlarged scope of offerings; changes in society itself have demanded training adapted increasingly to the individual need. In consequence, regimented training has tended to drop out and greater attention has been paid to student purposes and to preparation for the part that the student will play in the manifold activities of society following graduation.

All these changes have demanded more extensive and more adequate training on the part of all liberal arts colleges. There has developed a trend, in consequence, toward larger institutions equipped with more adequate facilities. Each institution has directed its attention increasingly to its relationship to the social order and has attempted to make a more extensive contribution than was required of it a short time before.

With these changes in general training there have occurred also changes in professional training. New professions have come into being, and with the application of scientific method to almost all activities there has occurred an up-grading of professions all along the line. Schools have been founded to give adequate professional training in many pursuits for which no formal training had been provided. Higher standard training on the part of the professions has required the working out of pre-professional training on the part of the liberal arts college. This has meant enlargement of offerings and the development of greater facilities for carrying these on. The single institution has been forced to expand its program and to acquire greater resources to make ever greater expansion possible. In the face of insistent demand for increased opportunities on the part of society and in the face of inadequate income the single institution has felt the pressure toward coordination as a means of providing more adequate offerings.

This dual necessity for more adequate general and professional training has emphasized the trend toward specialization. The structure of higher educational institutions has become, in consequence, increasingly complex. As a result of specialization there have been added new departments. From these departments there have been developed specialized faculties and schools, all members of the original institution. Out of the liberal arts college there has, thus, grown the typical American university, a group of professional schools with the college of liberal arts as a nucleus. For the various schools within the university there has been provided by the central organization many common facilities, but each school devoted to its differentiated purpose has specialized facilities of its own. These specialized facilities are supplemented where necessary by the common facilities of the whole institution. Specialization has been able to take place, even as in the case of the single department, because the specialized facilities of the differentiated school could be supplemented at will by the general offerings of the larger institution and by the specialized offerings of other schools within it.

To sum up, then, more adequate higher educational provision, which is insistently demanded by society, is made possible through more adequate facilities, which in turn are made possible through increased specialization, which depends upon the ability to supplement the specialized offerings, where necessary, from the offerings of other general or specialized programs.

Coordination of higher educational institutions results, in consequence, from the demand on these institutions for more adequate offerings. Unable as are all institutions to provide offerings of the scope and standard that are needed by the developing society, they are considering more and more the possibilities of coordination as a solution. Coordination is the result of the same trend that has led to institutional expansion.

Through coordination greater effectiveness is achieved for the offerings of the participating institution. By means of interchange of facilities, institutional offerings are supplemented, weak offerings are strengthened, the use of costly and specialized facilities belonging to one institution is made possible to another, and new offerings, which none of the institutions was in a position to provide alone, are developed.

Coordination has also been fostered through the increasing demand that has developed in society for social planning. Waste, both in talent and in money, has been seen to result from independent institutional enterprise in higher education. Serious doubts have been raised in the minds of constituencies and of the institutions themselves by the needless expense involved as a result of duplicated offerings and overhead. In addition, independent enterprise for more than one hundred years has led to conflicts of institutional interests and to competitive activities for both students and support.[14]

[14] For example, there occurs the following statement made by the Trustees of Williams College in 1818: "That since its (Williams College's) establishment in 1793, other colleges have sprung up about it and had almost wholly withdrawn the patronage from the North and West. That, owing to the want of support, its funds have become so reduced that the income falls short of the expenditures, and the Trustees are for this reason unable to maintain the institution in its present state, and enable it to compete with other colleges." Durfee, Calvin A., *A History of Williams College*, p. 150. A. Williams & Co. Boston, 1860.

In 1860 conflicts of institutional interests still presented a problem. The *Journal* of the General Conference of the Methodist Episcopal Church held in Buffalo, New York, speaks of the "undue multiplication of literary institutions, especially those of higher grade" (pp. 454-55). Editor, William L. Harris. Carleton and Lanahan, New York, 1860.

That the problem still faces higher education is indicated in Stockwell's statement, made in 1929: "We need to learn wherein our church colleges tend to overlap or to compete with each other and with other educational institutions in the area." Stockwell, Frederick, "Address of the Retiring President of the Council of Church Boards of Education." *Christian Education*, Vol. XII, No. 5, p. 267, February 1929.

CHAPTER II

Definition and Scope of Study

DEFINITIONS

AN ATTEMPT will be made to explain here the meaning with which certain terms are used in this study. Such explanation is felt to be necessary inasmuch as there has been found little uniformity in the use of these terms in the educational literature. Explanation of meanings will be of aid in indicating the scope of the study.

The term "agreement" refers to contracts, understandings, and connections established between higher institutions for the purpose of improving and enlarging their educational offerings. Agreements in some cases are very loose in character, involving simply an interchange of instruction and facilities; whereas in other cases they are extremely close, providing for cooperation all along the line. Under agreement participating institutions retain their separate identity, surrendering no powers granted under charters, and retain their separate corporate organization and their own boards of trustees.

The terms "consolidation" and "merger" differ from the term "agreement" as used in this study in that consolidations and mergers require the surrender of the institutional charter of one or both participating institutions. Consolidations and mergers result in integral organization, with a centering of control in the hands of a single board. In consequence, the consolidation and the merger necessitate the giving up of the separate corporate organization of one or both institutions and the doing away with their separate boards of trustees.

The terms "affiliation" and "federation" have been employed in the literature to mean combination through agreement. Neither term, whether in the United States or in Canada, however, has achieved a precise meaning with respect to the structure which is set up or the degree of cooperation established. Affiliation at one institution means quite a different type of cooperation from that at another. It has seemed desirable, therefore, to avoid confusion resulting from the use of this term. The use of the term affiliation has also been avoided in deference to a prejudice existing in certain quarters against it. Affiliation has been thought to imply a mother-daughter relationship between a stronger and a weaker institution. Such is very often not the case, but the relationship is a partnership between sovereign institutions and the equality under such a partnership is best expressed in the term agreement.

Another term which has been employed is "the cooperative arrangement." This term is acceptable but has been avoided because it is more awkward than the term agreement. Two terms have been used to indicate institutions taking part in agreements: "allied institutions" and "participating institutions."

The term "integration" is often employed in the literature dealing with agreements, consolidations, and mergers. No objection is raised to this term as indicating a trend toward combination. Agreements, of course, may result from disintegration: the breaking down of one unit integrally organized into several units, each under its own board of control.

The term "coordination" is employed to mean to harmonize or bring into a state of cooperation for mutual benefit. Where institutions are merged or consolidated, even though they lose their identity as separate institutions, this is referred to as coordination as well as when they achieve cooperation through agreement.

The term "interchange of students" is not to be confused with the term "transfer of students." Transfer of students involves discontinuance of attendance at one institution at the time the student enrolls at the other. Under interchange of students, the student continues to be enrolled at one while enrolling for courses at the other.

The term "interchange of faculty" is not to be confused with "exchange professorship." An exchange professor discontinues his service at the institution where he is primarily employed for the period of time that he gives service in the other institution. Under interchange of faculty, the faculty member serves both institutions at the same time. Neither agreements which provide solely for transfer of students nor agreements which provide solely for exchange professorships have been included in this study, inasmuch as it was felt that coordination established thereby was too loose to be of the same nature as that established in other agreements.

"Higher educational institutions" are those commonly designated as colleges, universities, and professional schools. A more precise interpretation of the term indicates institutions which require for admission to regular standing the satisfactory completion of a standard four-year secondary school course or its equivalent. This study has not found it possible to check the admission standards of institutions which have participated in agreements, and very possibly some of the schools of art, music, and theology do not conform to this standard.

Agreements with secondary schools, although occurring in some instances, have not been included in this study. Agreements with boards of education of a city educational system have also not been included. Furthermore, junior colleges have not been included among the institutions participating in agreements in that some of these enrolling students from the third year of the high school course, or giving as part of their regular programs high school courses, are obviously not higher educational institutions.

Finally, agreements with certain other types of institution have not been included. Such institutions are: botanical gardens, Christian associations, churches, clinics, galleries, hospitals, libraries, museums, and industrial research plants. Although certain universities have formed many agreements with institutions of these types, the agreements have not been included because these institutions are not formal higher educational agencies.

STATEMENT OF THE PROBLEM

As far as can be learned no investigation of inter-institutional agreements as a whole among higher educational institutions has been made. Almost without exception agreements have been developed independently in response to particular situations. The need has been felt for an inclusive investigation of this instrument of coordination inasmuch as it has been employed to a considerable extent in higher education. Specifically, answers are desired to the questions: how many agreements are in force, how these differ in character, and for what purposes they are employed. On the basis of these findings the study hopes to arrive at principles which will be of value in greater adaptation of the individual institution, in more extensive and higher quality provision of higher education for the area, and in the cooperative planning of higher education in the nation.

This study proposes seven problems for which answers are sought. The statement of each problem follows.

1. To what extent have inter-institutional agreements been employed among higher educational institutions? The answer to this question will attempt to list all agreements now in force. These will be examined to learn the form in which they are recorded; the number participated in by any one institution; the type of institutions participating in them; the enrollment of institutions participating in them; to what extent publicly supported institutions, Roman Catholic institutions, and Negro institutions have formed agreements; and the geographical location of institutions participating in agreements. Finally, abrogated agreements and agreements under consideration will be listed.

2. What conditions govern the formation of inter-institutional agreements? On the basis of the information afforded in the documents which have been received, there will be presented a discussion of those conditions which have appeared to be most influential in the formation of agreements. The conditions discussed will be: program, type, and size of participating institutions; proximity, location, and transportation facilities between participating institutions; prospect of financial saving, institutional recognition, and greater service for the area.

3. What changes in institutional structure and function result from participation in agreements? The answer to this question will treat of changes in: control, administration, faculty and facilities.

4. What provision has been set up for safeguarding institutional identity and powers under agreements? The answer to this question will treat of: retention of identity and powers of corporations; retention of control of property and finances; retention of control of programs; retention of control of students; integrity of charters; powers for modification and termination of agreements.

5. What values are sought under agreement? There will be considered: preservation and augmentation of institutional distinctive character; preservation of identity and powers under agreement; enlarged and increased offerings without loss to institutional programs; decreased institutional expense with the same or increased service; preservation and increase in standards of achievement; joint direction and supervision on administrative and instructional problems; the same or increased recognition for allied institutions; cooperative planning of higher education for the area.

6. What are characteristics of undesirable agreements?

7. What implications have agreements for cooperative planning of higher education?

PROCEDURE

There was first compiled a list of all agreements believed to be in force. This list was compiled from examination of catalogs and publications of colleges and universities; examination of reports and bulletins of educational and professional associations; examination of educational literature contained in journals and other works; letters from educational associations and foundations; interviews where possible with administrators of higher educational institutions; and interviews with officers of associations and foundations.

On the basis of this list a prepared letter was sent to one of each pair of institutions participating in an agreement. Records and copies of all agreements entered into by that institution with other higher educational institutions were requested. Where an original agreement had been modified, a copy of each draft was desired. Related papers which might throw light on conditions governing agreements, values involved, and advantages sought were also requested.

The response to this letter was gratifying, only one institution refusing to give the information desired and only seven failing to make any reply to the letter. In some cases the information was insufficient and another letter was sent to these institutions. Where information was still not obtained, the prepared letter was sent to the other institution participating in the agreement.

Finally, in order that no agreement should be omitted from this study because it was not included on the list which had been compiled, one hundred additional letters were sent to institutions where no agreement was known to be in existence. These institutions were selected on the basis of their location in large cities, their proximity to other institutions, their general type and character. They were felt to constitute a fair sampling of higher institutions not previously communicated with. Replies to this letter seemed to justify the belief that the list of institutions participating in agreements was reasonably complete.

SOURCES

The sources for this study have been documents treating of inter-institutional agreements. The major number of these documents were received directly from the institutions participating in agreements and were copies and records of the agreements. In some cases information was drawn from educational journals, bulletins, and historical studies. In a few instances the information already collected was supplemented by a personal interview with institutional administrators or the officers of foundations and associations.

CHAPTER III

Extent to Which Agreements Have Been Developed

NUMBER OF AGREEMENTS IN FORCE

How many agreements are known to have been consummated by higher educational institutions? Examination of the documents received early disclosed that there must be some common basis for reckoning the number of agreements before an answer to this question was possible. It was decided, therefore, to consider an agreement a connection, understanding, or contract between two independent higher institutions. In consequence, where a document provides for connections between three institutions, each enjoying a relationship with each of the others, this has been counted as three agreements. Where two institutions have formed agreements with a third but have, as a result, no recognized connection with each other, this has been counted as constituting only two agreements.

The list of inter-institutional agreements to be presented is designed to be inclusive within the limitations of this study. In the list there are included, therefore, agreements of widely differing intimacy. Clarification of this point is necessary because in many instances agreements of differing intimacy are listed side by side, or are listed as being formed with the same institution.

On the preliminary list which was compiled there appeared 117 agreements. Eighty-nine prepared letters were sent to institutions participating in these agreements. Replies were received from all but seven. Of the eighty-two institutions replying, one refused to give the information desired, one was no longer in existence, and fourteen replied that no agreements had been consummated inasmuch as the institutions specified were under the same board of control. In the case of four the agreements were temporary and could not be included. Where additional agreements were reported, these were added to the new list. In response to the one hundred letters sent to institutions at random, sixty-three replies were received. Four of these reported agreements, four others reported

TABLE I

INTER-INSTITUTIONAL AGREEMENTS IN OPERATION AMONG HIGHER EDUCATIONAL INSTITUTIONS

Atlanta University	1. Morehouse College
	2. Spelman College
Boston University	
School of Practical Arts and Letters	3. The Garland School
School of Theology	4. Episcopal Theological School
School of Theology	5. * Harvard Divinity School
School of Theology	6. Newton Theological Institution
Brown University	7. Rhode Island School of Design
University of California	8. California College of Pharmacy
	9. California School of Fine Arts
	10. Hastings College of the Law
Case School of Applied Science	11. Cleveland College
Catholic University of America	12. Catholic Sisters' College
	13. National Catholic School of Social Service
University of Chicago	14. Otho S. A. Sprague Memorial Institute
Yerkes Observatory	15. Perkins Observatory, Ohio Wesleyan University
Graduate Divinity School	16. Theological seminaries (the names of these seminaries were not furnished)
University of Cincinnati	17. Hebrew Union College
Teachers College	18. Cincinnati Conservatory of Music
	19. College of Law
Claremont Colleges	20. La Verne College
	21. Pomona College
	22. Scripps College
Clark University (Georgia)	23. Gammon Theological Seminary
Colorado College	24. Broadmoor Art Academy
Columbia University	25. Barnard College
	26. Bloomfield Theological Seminary
	27. The College of Pharmacy of the City of New York
	28. Drew Theological Seminary
	29. General Theological Seminary of the Protestant Episcopal Church
	30. Jewish Theological Seminary of America
	31. New York Post-Graduate Medical School and Hospital
	32. New York School of Social Work
	33. St. Joseph's Theological Seminary
	34. St. Stephen's College†,
	35. * Teachers College
	36. Theological Seminary of the Reformed Church in America
	37. Union Theological Seminary
Creighton University	38. Duchesne College
	39. St. Mary's College
University of Denver	40. Iliff School of Theology
Drury College	41. School of the Bible
Furman University	42. Greenville Woman's College
George Peabody College for Teachers	43. Graduate School of the Y. M. C. A.
	44. Scarritt College for Christian Workers
	45. * Vanderbilt University
Harvard University	* Boston University School of Theology
Graduate Divinity School	46. Episcopal Theological School
Graduate Divinity School	47. Newton Theological Institution
Graduate Divinity School	48. Tufts School of Theology
Graduate Divinity School	49. Fletcher School of Law and Diplomacy, Tufts College
	50. Massachusetts Institute of Technology
	51. Radcliffe College
Graduate School of Business Administration	52. Law School, Yale University
Hobart College	53. New York State Agricultural Experiment Station
Illinois College	54. Illinois Conservatory of Music
Iowa State A. & M. College	55. School of Music
University of Iowa	56. School of Religion
University of Kentucky	57. The College of the Bible
	58. * Transylvania College

† The name of St. Stephen's College was changed in May 1934 to Bard College.
* Agreements appearing twice but enumerated only once in Table I.

TABLE I (*concluded*)

Lawrence College
MacMurray College
University of Missouri
State University of Montana
Morehouse College

University of New Mexico
New York University
  School of Education
  School of Education
  School of Education
North Central College

Northwestern University

North Dakota Agricultural College
University of North Dakota
Ohio State University
University of Pennsylvania

  School of Education
  School of Education

  School of Education
  School of Education
  School of Fine Arts
University of Pittsburgh
  School of Education
Pomona College

Princeton University
St. Lawrence University

St. Louis University

Simmons College

University of Southern California

Teachers College, Columbia University

Transylvania College

Union University

Vanderbilt University

Vassar College
Western Reserve University

Wittenberg College
Yale University

59. Institute of Paper Chemistry
60. Illinois Conservatory of Music
61. The Bible College of Missouri
62. The Montana School of Religion
    * Atlanta University
63. Spelman College
64. School of American Research
65. National Academy of Design
66. Biblical Seminary of New York
67. Jewish School of Social Work
68. New York School of Social Work
69. Evangelical Theological Seminary (there is evidence that other seminaries have formed agreements with N.C.C.)
70. Garrett Biblical Institute
71. National College of Education
72. Western Theological Seminary
73. Wesley College
74. Wesley College
75. Perkins Observatory, Ohio Wesleyan University
76. Crozer Seminary
77. Episcopal Divinity School
78. The Thomas W. Evans Museum and Dental Institute
79. Drexel Institute
80. Illman Training School for Kindergarten and Primary Teachers
81. School of Design for Women
82. School of Industrial Art
83. Pennsylvania Academy of Fine Arts

84. Pittsburgh Musical Institute, Inc.
    * Claremont Colleges
85. Scripps College
86. Princeton Theological Seminary
87. Brooklyn Law School
88. New York State School of Agriculture
89. Theological School
90. Fontbonne College
91. Maryville College
92. Webster College
93. Bouve School of Physical Education
94. Lowthorpe School of Landscape Architecture
95. College of Dentistry
96. Los Angeles University of International Relations
97. Barnard College
98. Institute of Musical Art
99. Teachers Institute, Jewish Theological Seminary of America
100. The College of the Bible
    * University of Kentucky
101. Union College
102. Albany College of Pharmacy
103. Albany Law School
104. Albany Medical College
    * George Peabody College for Teachers
105. Graduate School of the Y. M. C. A.
106. Scarritt College for Christian Workers
107. Sarah Lawrence College
108. Adelbert College
109. Cleveland College
110. Cleveland Institute of Music
111. Cleveland School of Architecture
112. Cleveland School of Art
113. Dayton Art Institute
114. Berkeley Divinity School
    * Harvard Graduate School of Business Administration
115. Witwatersrand University, South Africa

types of association that did not fulfill the specifications for agreements, and fifty-five replied that no agreement existed.

The list which was finally compiled consists of 115 agreements. These are presented in Table I. Where possible in this table the institution which is larger and which gives general training is placed in the left-hand column, whereas the smaller and more specialized institution appears in the right-hand column. In order that institutions in the right-hand column may include all institutions with which those in the left-hand column have consummated agreements, certain agreements have been repeated twice. In such cases an asterisk is placed before the name of the institution on the right and such agreements have been included only once in the enumeration.

Where agreements have been formed with a specific school within a university and not with the university as a whole, the name of the school has been included except where privileges have been opened to a number of other schools of the university as well. In some cases privileges are evidently less restricted than here indicated.

METHODS OF REPORTING AGREEMENTS

How were inter-institutional agreements reported by the institutions participating in them? The methods of reporting agreements cast light on the manner in which agreements are recorded in the various institutions. Table II indicates that 65 agreements, or 57 per cent of those reported, furnished copies of written contracts, corporation votes sanctioning agreements, or charters and by-laws. There is indication, therefore, that more than half the number of agreements have been acted upon formally and that there exist exact records of the terms of these agreements.

A very much larger proportion of agreements than those represented in these figures, however, have received formal action and are recorded more or less completely by the participating institutions. Included among agreements reported by catalog announcement are those where institutions failed to answer the letter of inquiry. It seems not unlikely that some of those institutions failed to reply because of uncertainty as to how the desired information was to be used. Others for the same reason furnished catalog announcements or gave a general description of agreements when they might have sent copies of the documents themselves. There seems little doubt from the replies accompanying certain documents that there was considerable hesitancy about supplying the desired information.

TABLE II

METHOD OF REPORTING 115 AGREEMENTS ENTERED INTO BY HIGHER
EDUCATIONAL INSTITUTIONS

Method of Reporting	Number Reported
Text of charters or by-laws setting forth provisions of agreement	7
Text of contract signed by participating institutions	44
Text of vote of board of trustees of one institution or the other sanctioning agreement	14
Letter from responsible administrative officer describing agreement	31
Catalog statement describing agreement	19
Total	115

Note: Where an agreement was reported in two ways, as, for instance, by text of contract and by letter, it is recorded under the heading which appears above the other in Table II.

On the other hand, letters were received from certain administrators who stated that to their knowledge no formal contract had ever been consummated. They stated that the agreements in question had been developed from an exchange of letters or as a result of interviews. Copies of such letters and memoranda were received in three cases; in other instances the administrator described the nature of the agreement and the practice followed under it. In one case an administrator acknowledged that there was an understanding with another institution but advised that, inasmuch as he was unaware of the precise terms of this understanding, a communication be addressed to the other institution. Some agreements appeared to be merely an extension of certain privileges to all institutions of a particular type whose students might wish to avail themselves of them. This courtesy having once been extended had never been withdrawn and, in consequence, was looked upon as still in operation. From these reports the conclusion seems well founded that agreements should be accurately recorded and that they should be revised at periodic intervals or terminated when they have ceased to be of advantage.

NUMBER OF AGREEMENTS FORMED BY A SINGLE INSTITUTION

The question was raised early in the study whether agreements tended to be grouped around certain institutions. In Table III it is seen that 102 institutions have participated in only one agreement. Of those participating in more than one agreement, 24 have entered into two agreements, 10 into three agreements, 4 into four agreements, 1 into five agreements, 2 into eight agreements, and 1 into

TABLE III

PRACTICE OF HIGHER EDUCATIONAL INSTITUTIONS OF PARTICIPATING IN MORE THAN ONE AGREEMENT

Agreements Participated In	Number of Institutions	Number of Agreements
13 agreements	1	13
8 agreements	2	16
5 agreements	1	5
4 agreements	4	16
3 agreements	10	30
2 agreements	24	48
1 agreement	102	102
Total agreements		230
Less one half, since two institutions participate in one agreement....		115

thirteen agreements. Reference to Table I reveals that a very large proportion of the institutions participating in but one agreement are either professional schools or colleges of liberal arts, whereas a large proportion of the institutions which have formed more than one agreement are universities. The indication is that the institution which offers several specialized programs by its very nature finds it beneficial to enter into agreements with several other institutions each of which is in position to supplement a part of its varied offerings. It also appears to be a justified conclusion that where an institution offers a single specialized program an agreement with one other institution in general is sufficient for its needs. This point of view is borne out by the fact that agreements formed with universities, as indicated in Table I, are frequently formed with a particular school within the university, and not with the university as a whole. For example, a theological school of a university forms an agreement with another theological school and the school of home economics of a university forms an agreement with an independent school of home economics. Thus a university tends to form several agreements, whereas an independent professional school tends to form only one.

Reference to Table I indicates that certain types of professional school have participated in large numbers of agreements. The question is therefore relevant whether agreements are limited in their usefulness to certain types of higher institution.

There does not appear to be evidence from examination of Table IV that the field for the formation of inter-institutional agreements is limited to any one type or to several types of institution. Agreements have been formed not only by many types of professional school but also by colleges for men, colleges for women, coeducational colleges, and universities.

TABLE IV

TYPES OF HIGHER EDUCATIONAL INSTITUTION PARTICIPATING IN 115
INTER-INSTITUTIONAL AGREEMENTS

Types of Higher Institution	Number Participating
Agriculture	4
Archeology	1
Architecture and Art	12
Astronomy	3
Business	1
Coeducational colleges	18
Dentistry	2
Engineering	4
Home economics	2
International relations	1
Law	5
Law and diplomacy	1
Medicine	3
Colleges for men	7
Music	7
Pharmacy	3
Social work	4
Teachers colleges	19
Theology and schools of religion	46
Colleges for women	16
Universities, as a unit	71
Total institutions	230

The term "type of higher institution" is not a precise term in that it indicates not only professional schools, colleges, and universities but also other kinds of higher institutions, such as institutions for

Negroes, public institutions, and denominational institutions. It may also indicate urban institutions, foreign institutions, and the like. These were not included in Table IV because to do so would necessitate duplication. It is proposed, therefore, to discuss separately the extent to which these types of institution have formed agreements.

Four agreements listed in Table I have been participated in by Negro institutions. Of the eight institutions participating, three are universities (Atlanta University has formed two agreements and Clark University one), two are colleges for men, two are colleges for women, and one is a theological seminary.

Only two types of denominational institution will be discussed here inasmuch as the term "denominational college" as applied to many Protestant institutions depends on interpretation. Roman Catholic institutions have participated in eight agreements. The Catholic University of America has formed two, Creighton University two, and St. Louis University three. In addition, St. Joseph's

TABLE V

TYPES OF PRIVATELY SUPPORTED HIGHER EDUCATIONAL INSTITUTION PARTICIPATING IN
AGREEMENTS WITH PUBLIC INSTITUTIONS

Types of Private Higher Institution	Number Participating
Archeology	1
Art	1
Astronomy	1
Coeducational colleges	2
Law	2
Music	3
Pharmacy	1
Theology and schools of religion	7
Universities	1
	—
Total private institutions participating in agreements with public institutions	19

seminary of the Roman Catholic Church, at Yonkers, New York, has formed an agreement with Columbia University. In these agreements, besides the universities and seminary mentioned there participate five colleges for women, one coeducational college, and one college for social work. Jewish institutions have also participated in agreements. The Jewish Theological Seminary of America has formed an agreement with Columbia University and an agreement with Teachers College, Columbia University. The Hebrew Union College has formed an agreement with the University of Cincinnati.

Nineteen agreements have been formed by publicly supported institutions. Of these, public universities have formed thirteen, schools of agriculture three, an agricultural experiment station one, and teachers colleges of publicly supported universities two. Agreements entered into by publicly supported institutions, although not as numerous as agreements between private institutions, show a broad range of application. Table V indicates that they have been formed with nine types of private institution. It is also of interest to note that one of these types of private institution is the theological school and school of religion, and that public institutions have formed seven agreements with these.

GEOGRAPHICAL LOCATION OF INSTITUTIONS CONSUMMATING AGREEMENTS

Are agreements limited to institutions located in one section of the United States, or in a few sections, or have institutions in all parts of the United States formed agreements? Table VI shows the distribution of 115 agreements according to nine geographical

TABLE VI

NUMBER OF INTER-INSTITUTIONAL AGREEMENTS FOUND IN NINE
GEOGRAPHICAL DIVISIONS OF THE UNITED STATES

Geographical Divisions	Number of Agreements
New England States	16
Middle Atlantic States	39
East North Central States	25
West North Central States	8
South Atlantic States	7
East South Central States	8
West South Central States	0
Mountain States	3
Pacific States	9
Total agreements	115

divisions of the country. Evidence from Table VI indicates that institutions participating in agreements are located in all divisions of the United States except one, the West South Central States.

It should be added also that, except for the foreign institution listed, both parties to agreements are located in every case in the same section of the country.

Have agreements been formed in most cases by colleges and universities whose enrollments are large or have they been formed by large numbers of institutions whose enrollments are small? Table VII (page 37) presents the enrollment range of colleges and universities participating in agreements, the number of institutions of each enrollment which participate, and the number of agreements which institutions of each enrollment have formed. Where agreements have been formed by a professional school within a university, that university was included in the number listed. Enrollments for separate professional schools, however, have not been included.

The enrollment statistics for colleges and universities which formed the basis for Table VII are those reported in the *Biennial Survey of Education for 1928-1930*, Volume II, Chapter IV. In this survey no enrollment statistics were found for Claremont Colleges exclusive of those for Pomona and Scripps. The several enrollments of the Corporate Colleges of St. Louis University were not presented separately from those for the university. This is also the case for the two colleges linked by agreement to Creighton University. The statistics for these colleges were therefore not included in Table VII.

Table VII indicates that colleges and universities participating in agreements range from institutions with fewer than 500 students to institutions with more than 32,000 students. Agreements do not appear to be limited to institutions of either small or large enrollment.

ABROGATED AGREEMENTS

The investigation of inter-institutional agreements indicated that a certain number of agreements once in force had been discontinued. Information has been difficult to secure for most of these cases and has had to be obtained from references in institutional histories, catalog announcements, annual reports, and other literature dealing with higher education. For this reason the list of ten to be presented cannot be regarded as complete. Doubtless there are many others which might be added. Failure to find references has been doubtless due to the fact that where an agreement was abrogated it was henceforth regarded as of little importance.

Agreements which have been abrogated were formed between: Illinois College and the University of Chicago;[1] the College of Physicians and Surgeons and Columbia University;[2] the National Academy of Design and Columbia University;[3] Columbia University and Yale University, providing a training course for foreign service;[4] Brown University and S. Dunstan's College of Sacred Music;[5] Denison University and Shepardson College;[6] Harvard University and the Andover Theological Seminary;[7] Harvard University and the Massachusetts Institute of Technology;[8] Mount Morris College and the Bethany Biblical Seminary;[9] Westminster College and Synodical College;[10] St. Louis University and Chaminade College.[11]

The same difficulties which handicapped the making of a list of abrogated agreements beset also the attempt to find out the causes for abrogation. Some of the more significant causes undoubtedly are: the closing of one of the participating institutions; the merging of the two institutions; provisions of institutional charters invalidating the terms of the agreement; fear that the agreement involved loss of institutional independence; fear that the agreement involved loss of standing for one or the other institution; the development of facilities in one or the other institution, making the agreement no longer desirable.

From this list it is seen that agreements may be terminated as a result of a merger between the two institutions. It is also seen

[1] Rammelkamp, C. H. Centennial History of Illinois College, p. 458. Yale University Press, New Hav 1928.
[2] History of Colur ..u University, 1754-1904, p. 243. Columbia University Press, New York, 1905.
[3-4] Butler, Nicholas M., Annual Report, pp. 31, 32, Columbia University, 1906.
[5] Bulletin of Brown University, November 1931.
[6] Shepardson, Francis W., Denison University, 1831-1931, A Centennial History, pp. 364-65. Granville, Ohio, 1931.
[7] Morison, S. E., Development of Harvard University. Chapter entitled "The Theological School, 1896-1928," p. 446. Harvard University Press, 1930.
[8] Ibid., p. 446.
[9] Bulletin of Mount Morris College, April, May, June, 1931.
[10] Morgan, F. G., "Integration in Higher Education." Unpublished dissertation for the Ph.D. degree, University of South Carolina, 1928.
[11] Bulletin of St. Louis University, February 1931.

that agreements may be abrogated because the cooperation itself has broken down. In addition, abrogation may result from the need of forming a new agreement better adapted to the participating institutions. An example of this practice is the agreement between Harvard University and the Massachusetts Institute of Technology. The first agreement providing for close cooperation could not be carried out and, in consequence, a new agreement was consummated wherein the relationship was extremely loose.

The relationship between institutions changes from year to year as the needs of the institutions vary. In almost all cases this change in relationship takes place under the terms of the original contract. Where the change, however, is pronounced, modification of the agreement is made in recognition of the new needs which have developed. Only where the original relationship was profoundly altered or where the contract itself was inadequate in the beginning does abrogation take place, leading to the abandonment of the cooperation which was established or to the consummation of a new agreement.

AGREEMENTS NOT YET CONSUMMATED

In certain cases it was reported that agreements were now under consideration and that they would soon be put in force. On page 4 of this study two such agreements were referred to. Mention was made of the attempt to coordinate graduate instruction in the Philadelphia region and attention was called to the study now under way for coordinating the offerings of the University of Chicago and Northwestern University. The President of the Case School of Applied Science reported that an agreement had been approved by the Case School and Western Reserve University for a permanent cooperative organization and that this would soon be put in force.

SUMMARY

One hundred fifteen inter-institutional agreements have been listed in this chapter. Although this number of agreements is not large, as compared with the number of higher educational institutions in existence, there is evidence that the inter-institutional agreement for coordinating the work of higher educational institutions has been employed to a considerable extent.

From examination of agreements at present in operation it is evident that agreements are not limited to particular types of institution. Not only have colleges, universities, and many types of professional school formed agreements, but agreements have been consummated by Negro as well as white institutions, by public as well as private institutions, by Roman Catholic and Jewish as well as Protestant institutions. Furthermore, the agreements are not limited to institutions of any particular enrollment size, nor are they restricted to any geographical section of the country.

Examination of agreements has indicated that agreements differ widely in the degree of cooperation which they establish, that the same institution frequently forms more than one agreement, and that a proportion of the agreements listed are imperfectly recorded by the institutions which make use of them. Finally, a list was presented of abrogated agreements and mention was made of certain agreements about to be put in force.

CHAPTER IV

Conditions Governing the Formation of Agreements

THIS chapter will discuss certain conditions which have appeared to play a determining part in the formation of inter-institutional agreements. These conditions are: program, type, and size of participating institutions; their proximity, location and the transportation facilities between them; the prospect of financial saving for one or both institutions; the prospect of greater institutional recognition; and, finally, the prospect of greater service to the area in which they are located.

PROGRAMS OF PARTICIPATING INSTITUTIONS

There seems reason to believe that the offerings of participating institutions are extremely important factors in the formation of agreements. Institutions whose programs are identical seldom form agreements. Agreements are formed by colleges, universities, and professional schools whose offerings to a greater or less degree supplement each other. This is particularly true in the case of the agreement entered into by a professional school. The professional school increases the range and effectiveness of its own program by interchange of facilities with another institution. In some cases the programs of the allied institutions differ very slightly and the interchange is small. In other cases, where there is, for instance, no integrally organized professional school of a certain type in a university, the agreement may constitute the allied professional school, the professional school of the university. The program of the professional school is then supplemented to a large degree through the other offerings of the university.

This view that the opportunities for supplementation of offerings determine to a great extent the formation of agreements is reinforced by the fact that a university does not contract an agreement with a professional school provided the university can adequately offer the program given by this institution. Furthermore, colleges and universities do not form agreements with two or more professional schools affording identical offerings. Agreements entered into by several theological schools with a particular university are no exception to this principle. The theological schools represent different denominations and the different character of each enables it to make its separate contribution. The agreements entered into by New York University with the New York School of Social Work and with the Jewish School of Social Work supplement the offering of the University School of Education in different ways. The Jewish School of Social Work as part of its training acquaints the student with Jewish custom and background in order that he may deal more effectively with Jewish charity cases. The School of Industrial Art and the School of Design for Women make distinctive contributions to the program offered by the School of Education of the University of Pennsylvania.

Often where two professional schools offer similar programs the demand for coordination leads to their consolidation rather than to the formation of an agreement. Thus, to avoid duplication between a professional school integrally organized within a university and an independent professional school outside the university the two schools are frequently merged prior to the formation of an agreement, the agreement then taking place between the university and the consolidated institution. Such was the case in the agreement between the dental school of the University of Pennsylvania and the Thomas W. Evans Museum and Institute Society. The University continued to give only those dental courses not offered by the Evans Society. It also provided courses in related departments or schools which were required to round out the training given by the consolidated institution. A somewhat similar example occurred in the case of the schools of music of Illinois and MacMurray Colleges. Through an agreement these were merged into the Illinois Conservatory of Music, under the management of the Board of MacMurray College assisted by an advisory council made up of representatives of both colleges. This new institution maintains relationships with both colleges.

Agreements are not formed where the relationship between two institutions would lead to duplication of their entire programs. There may be duplication under agreement in many courses, but it is almost always the case that the agreement insures different total programs or different emphases. This is particularly true in the case of agreements formed by colleges with other colleges or universities. Although giving frequently practically the same course, these institutions provide for a different type of student, specialize in certain departments, or give training under different circumstances, and this has the effect of joining institutions whose programs are different. An example is St. Stephen's College which differs from Columbia College in having a small enrollment, in being located in rural surroundings, and in being denominational in character. The agreement formed between Atlanta University and Morehouse and Spelman Colleges provides that graduate instruction be limited to the University. The two colleges serve different groups of students, one undergraduate men and the other undergraduate women. Scripps and Pomona Colleges differ in the students they serve, the former being an undergraduate college for women and the latter an undergraduate coeducational college.

Difference in offering seems to be a factor, therefore, in the formation of agreements. This indicates that the desire for mere bigness is not the determining factor leading to agreements, but that agreements are entered into in order to enlarge and improve the offerings of the participating institutions.

TYPE OF HIGHER INSTITUTION

Where a certain type of higher institution has formed a large proportion of the agreements listed, there is the probability that it has found agreements serviceable, and that this type of institution represents a factor fostering the formation of agreements. As will be seen from Table IV, the largest number of agreements have been formed with universities. This is what might be expected inasmuch as the university, offering many types of training, can profit from association with many different institutions. Other types of institution will be discussed in turn.

Theological Seminaries and Schools of Religion

More than one third of the agreements listed have been participated in by seminaries. There seem to be several reasons for this. In the first place, the seminary and the denominational college have frequently been founded by the same sectarian group and pursue the same aim, the training of religious leadership. In consequence, students of the college very naturally avail themselves of the offerings of the seminary, and students of the seminary find advantage in completing their general education in the college.

Combined courses have been worked out permitting the taking of two degrees in a shortened number of years. Interchange of facilities has held out advantages to both the college and the seminary.

In the second place, a single university has found it desirable to form agreements with several seminaries. These seminaries differ in denominational affiliation and the students of the university representing many different denominations are thus afforded opportunities for work in institutions of their particular faith. Columbia University has formed seven such agreements: one with a Catholic seminary, one with a Jewish seminary, and five with Protestant seminaries. Harvard has four such agreements, Boston University three, Northwestern, the University of Pennsylvania, and Vanderbilt two each, and Chicago several. In the case of Columbia and Northwestern the university has no seminary integrally organized under its board. In the case of Boston, Chicago, Harvard, Vanderbilt, and Yale, however, the university has its own theological school. The university also profits from the presence of theological students on its campus and in its courses. These bring different points of view and different aims. Not only private universities so profit but also public universities. Table V shows that seven agreements have been participated in by public institutions with seminaries or schools of religion. Mathews remarks that the seminary student gains from the widely differing contacts found on the state university campus and also believes that the state university profits from the earnest type of men attracted to the faculty of the seminary and to its student body.[1] The movement to bring religious influence and denominational teaching to the state university campus has found expression in the past few years in the development of schools of religion. This institution is unique in that it brings together into one program the teaching of the various denominations. At the University of Iowa there has been established under a separate board of trustees a school of religion in which participate Roman Catholics, Jews, and seven different Protestant denominations. A similar institution is the Montana School of Religion established at the State University of Montana.

A final reason for the development of agreements with seminaries is, of course, the desire to place the university resources at the disposal of the seminary student. The seminary student finds his

---

[1] Mathews, Shailer, "The State University and the Theological Seminary." *Religious Education*, Vol. IV, pp. 182-83, June 1909.

opportunities enlarged through courses in allied fields, such as philosophy and political science. In many cases university courses are opened to the seminary student without charge. This practice is in line with the practice in the theological seminary of providing training at as little charge as possible. It has been customary to relieve the theological student to a large degree of the cost of his training. Through agreement the university cooperates in this practice.

Colleges for Teachers

Nineteen agreements have been formed by teachers colleges, some by independent institutions and some by schools of education within a university. The many types of professional training required in the preparation of teachers, demanding a knowledge of subject matter as well as of the principles of education, have fostered agreements not only with universities and colleges but also with certain types of professional school. Agreements have been formed with schools of art, music, social work, and theology. Through agreements combined courses have been worked out to the mutual advantage of these institutions. Growing recognition of the value of systematic training in education would seem to indicate that there is opportunity for closer alliance between the teachers college, the liberal arts college, various types of professional school, and the university as well.

Schools of Art and Music

Twelve schools of art and architecture and seven schools of music participate in agreements. A number of influences have brought this about. Outstanding is the contribution made by such institutions to the program of the liberal arts college, a contribution seldom possible to as great an extent through a college department because of limited resources and personnel. Part of this contribution is the lectures and exhibits of general interest open to the members of the college as a result of this association. Similar advantages in the college are enjoyed by the members of the school of art or music. Another advantage is the training course which is often worked out by both institutions, leading to a certificate or degree qualifying teachers of music or art. In such cases the theoretical work is given in the college and the applied work in the professional school. Still other advantages may impel such agreements. Through cooperation with an existing school of music the college may obtain expert instruction for its glee club and choruses.

Colleges for Women

Many agreements with women's colleges have been consummated for the same reasons which led to the consummation of agreements with coeducational colleges or colleges for men. Women's colleges have joined in agreements with universities or professional schools or other colleges for the purpose of improving and enlarging their offerings. In certain cases, however, the women's college, because of its distinctive character, has been a factor in the formation of agreements and for this reason deserves attention.

Women's colleges have participated in sixteen agreements. Of this number four have been consummated as part of a plan for coordinate men's and women's institutions. Two of the earliest coordinate women's colleges are Barnard and Radcliffe, which formed agreements at the time of their founding a few years before the opening of the century. The relationship established in the case of the former was through a contract signed by itself and Columbia University; in the case of the latter the relationship with Harvard University is provided for in the statutes of the College. Provision is made in the charter of Catholic Sisters' College for its relationship to the Catholic University of America. Spelman College is the only one of the four which was in existence prior to the formation of the agreement. Through this agreement, Atlanta University undertook to provide all graduate instruction; Morehouse College became the undergraduate college for men and Spelman College became the undergraduate college for women.

Coordinate colleges for women have been worked out as a substitute for coeducation. They are the result of the increasing demand that the opportunities already provided for men be extended to the members of the other sex. The women's college is located on its own campus, where it conducts its own program, similar in most respects to that in the men's college; but it conducts its separate classes of the same standard in all respects as those on the men's campus and it enjoys separate activities such as are possible to an institution enrolling only women.

In general, the object of instituting this form of organization through agreement is the desire to provide institutional autonomy and limited financial responsibility. Interests sponsoring women's higher education are glad to retain voice in the management of the woman's college and they are also glad to have the freedom to develop differentiated curricula adapted to the needs of women students. On the other hand, it seems probable that, in placing the woman's college under a separate board of control, universities were influenced by skepticism which at one time existed concerning the ability of a woman's college to maintain a program of high standard. They were also influenced by the desire to be relieved of financial obligation for the maintenance of the college. The securing of endowment and gifts for women's higher education has been recognized as presenting a different problem from that of securing gifts and endowment for men's higher education. These financial aspects of the problem may lose importance as time goes on. The desire to continue separate management and separate control for institutions where separate education is maintained for the sexes but where a certain cooperation has been established seems as influential and to have every chance to continue as influential as formerly.

SIZE OF HIGHER INSTITUTIONS

Table VII indicates that all sizes of colleges and universities participate in agreements. Colleges and universities vary from enrollment less than 500 students to enrollment over 32,000 students. The smallest college which participates in an agreement is St. Stephen's with 132 students, and the largest university is New York University with 33,101 students.[2] If the enrollment of separately controlled professional schools is included, the smallest participating in an agreement is the Berkeley Divinity School, which enrolls 27 students, and the largest is Teachers College, Columbia University, which enrolls 6,788 students. These statistics, presented in Table VII, are distorted in the step intervals by the fact that the enrollment for the entire university is recorded in the case where one of its schools participates in an agreement. The range in enrollment among participant institutions, however, is not affected by this distortion. The largest university participating as a unit in an agreement continues to be New York University because of its agreement with the National Academy of Design. Agreements

[2] Enrollment statistics taken from the *Biennial Survey of Education, 1928-1930*, Vol. II, Chap. IV. United States Department of the Interior, Office of Education Bulletin (1931), No. 20.

cannot be said, therefore, to be limited to any one size or enrollment of institutions.

TABLE VII

ENROLLMENT FOR 55 COLLEGES AND UNIVERSITIES PARTICIPATING IN INTER-INSTITUTIONAL AGREEMENTS AND NUMBER OF AGREEMENTS FORMED

Enrollment	Number of Institutions	Number of Agreements
32,000–34,000	1	4
18,000–20,000	1	3
14,000–16,000	3	19
12,000–14,000	1	2
10,000–12,000	4	9
9,000–10,000	2	16
5,000– 6,000	3	5
4,000– 5,000	2	3
3,000– 4,000	2	6
2,000– 3,000	3	4
1,000– 2,000	15	23
500– 1,000	5	7
– 500	13	17
Totals	55	118

In the effort to find out whether there is a tendency for large institutions to form more agreements than small institutions, Table VIII was constructed. This table shows that the institution with large enrollment forms a greater percentage of agreements than the institution with small enrollment. This is what might be expected inasmuch as the large institution is the university, and the university with its many offerings finds many opportunities to cooperate with neighboring institutions.

On the other hand, Table VII indicates that the number of colleges and universities in the step intervals for larger enrollment is smaller than in the step intervals for smaller enrollment. It is evident, then, that although colleges and universities participating in agreements individually form more agreements if they are large, as a total group they form fewer agreements than colleges and universities participating in agreements which have small enrollments. Thus, the conclusion is that agreements are serviceable to the small college or university as well as to the large university.

This conclusion is of importance because of the bearing which it has on the life and future of the small college. Many writers

TABLE VIII

PERCENTAGE OF AGREEMENTS FORMED BY COLLEGES AND UNIVERSITIES
OF DIFFERENT ENROLLMENTS

Enrollment	Percentage of Agreements
32,000–34,000	4.00
18,000–20,000	3.00
14,000–16,000	6.34
12,000–14,000	2.00
10,000–12,000	2.25
9,000–10,000	8.00
5,000– 6,000	1.67
4,000– 5,000	1.50
3,000– 4,000	3.00
2,000– 3,000	1.34
1,000– 2,000	1.53
500– 1,000	1.40
– 500	1.30

have claimed that the independent small college cannot endure. The problem of the small college is widespread in American higher education. In 1930 unpublished compilations of the U. S. Office of Education stated that there were in existence throughout the country 176 four-year colleges with annual enrollments of less than 200 students.[3] Such institutions cannot hope to offer as extensive or adequate a program to meet the needs of a liberal arts education as is being offered by their neighboring larger institutions. The small college is faced with greater competition than ever before in its history. It must continue to give a four-year curriculum at the same time that universities and teachers colleges offer professional curricula beginning at the third year of the college course, and while the junior college is taking students from its first two years.[4] These other institutions are undermining the unit of instruction offered by the liberal arts college.

It is claimed by many that the small college independent of the large university cannot survive and that even the better endowed small college must eventually close its doors.[5] Over thirty years ago

[3] Hill, D. S. and Kelly, F. J., *Economy in Higher Education*, p. 59. The Carnegie Foundation for the Advancement of Teaching, New York, 1933.

[4] Reeves, Floyd W., "The Liberal Arts College." *The Journal of Higher Education*, Vol. I, No. 7, p. 378, 1930.

[5] Bell, B. I., "Report of the Warden of St. Stephen's College." *Annual Report*, Columbia University, 1929, p. 452.

President Harper pointed out the hazards of the small college in an illuminating address[6] in which he made his famous prediction stating that many small colleges would have to close their doors or change their status, becoming junior colleges or secondary schools. In the same address he held out the possibility of "federating" the small college with the large university and pointed out ten advantages which might accrue to the college from such association.

President Butler, in 1930, calls attention to the fact that the small college receives many benefits from coordination with a stronger neighboring institution.[7] Its offering may be enlarged and its scholarship stimulated. There are also made possible for its students and faculty a great variety of contacts through coordination, and there are obtained the aid and direction of the stronger institution in the conduct of its educational program. At the same time there is preserved its legal and financial independence under agreement. The small college is not to be thought of as a possession of the stronger institution but as an ally, both institutions cooperating in the provision of a more adequate program for the area and its constituency. Finally, President Blaisdell points out that agreements entered into by the small college enable it to preserve its distinctive character, its traditions, its loyalties, its campus, and its own institutional life. Such agreements enable groups of small colleges to be constituted side by side, thus forming a cooperative whole which affords many of the advantages of such a group organized within a university.[8]

The small college, then, is a factor determining the formation of agreements. Of course, agreements have been worked out in many different ways, providing for greater or less cooperation. Table VII indicates that thirteen colleges and universities with enrollment under 500 students and five more with enrollment less than 1,000 students have formed agreements. To this number must be added the three colleges allied to St. Louis University and the two colleges allied to Creighton University. The enrollment of these five insti-

[6] Harper, W. R., "The Situation of the Small College." An Address given in Charleston, South Carolina, July 10, 1900, before the National Education Association. Included in *The Trend in Higher Education*, pp. 388-89. The University of Chicago Press, Chicago, 1905.

[7] Butler, Nicholas Murray, *Annual Report*, p. 33. Columbia University, 1930.

[8] Blaisdell, J. A., "Claremont Colleges: Some Educational Purposes and Results." A Paper Presented at a Meeting of the Association of American Colleges, Washington, D. C., January 15, 1930. Page 6 of reprint from *Association of American Colleges Bulletin*, Vol. XVI, No. I, March 1930.

tutions is not included in Table VII inasmuch as statistics for them were not presented separately from those for their universities in the *1928-1930 Biennial Survey of Education*. Assuming that these five institutions are small in enrollment, the number of small colleges and universities forming agreements is twenty-three. This number is not large, compared with the number of professional schools which have formed agreements with other higher institutions. However, the small college is a factor and may well become a more considerable one in the fostering of agreements as coordination in future receives greater emphasis.

PROXIMITY OF HIGHER INSTITUTIONS

How much influence has proximity in the formation of inter-institutional agreements? With the exception of a few agreements to be noted, all agreements have been formed between institutions located less than fifteen miles from each other. In many cases, participant institutions are located in the same city or in the same metropolitan area. Sometimes they are located on adjoining campuses, as in the case of George Peabody College for Teachers and Vanderbilt University. They may be located on the same campus, as in the case of the Bible College of Missouri and the University of Missouri or the College of the Bible and Transylvania College.

The following instances are cases of agreements between institutions located at a distance (the mileage which is given is only approximate): The Perkins Observatory, Ohio Wesleyan University, participates in an agreement with the Yerkes Observatory, University of Chicago, 490 miles distant. The Brooklyn Law School is 320 miles from St. Lawrence University, Canton, New York. The Yale Law School is separated from the Harvard Graduate School of Business Administration by 160 miles. St. Stephen's College at Annandale-on-Hudson is 95 miles from Columbia University. Wesley College, Grand Forks, North Dakota, is 90 miles from the North Dakota Agricultural College. The University of New Mexico at Albuquerque and the School of American Research at Santa Fé are 60 miles distant from each other. Columbia University is 45 miles distant from New Brunswick, New Jersey, where is located the Theological Seminary of the Reformed Church in America, and is 30 miles distant from Drew Theological Seminary at Madison, New Jersey. These eight agreements, together with the one formed with a foreign institution, indicate that, whereas agreements are possible between institutions a considerable distance apart, such agreements have been developed to a very limited extent.

Proximity seems to be a determining factor in the formation of agreements, especially where there is provision for frequent interchange of faculty and facilities. Proximity plays a minor part in agreements which provide solely for coordination of control or administration. Where students attend a second institution for a considerable period, as part of their course at the first institution, proximity ceases to be significant.

GEOGRAPHICAL AND URBAN LOCATION

Agreements, it was pointed out in Table VI, have been formed in all sections of the country with the exception of the West South Central States. They have been found, however, in greatest numbers in the East and North. Here also is found the greatest density of population. Examination of the density of population for all sections of the country indicates that it in itself is not a determinant for formation of agreements. It seems instead that where high density of population is found, as indicated in Table IX, other factors also occur which have led to the formation of agreements.

In regions where high density of population is reported, there is

TABLE IX

DENSITY OF POPULATION IN NINE GEOGRAPHICAL DIVISIONS OF THE UNITED STATES AND THE NUMBER OF AGREEMENTS FORMED

Geographical Divisions	Density	Number of Agreements
New England States	270.6	16
Middle Atlantic States	338.9	39
East North Central States	109.3	25
West North Central States	24.1	8
South Atlantic States	77.8	5*
East South Central States	55.7	8
West South Central States	34.6	0
Mountain States	5.4	3
Pacific States	23.3	9
Total agreements		113*

* Owing to the fact that its density of population is so great that to include it would distort the figures, the District of Columbia was not included in the statistics representing the South Atlantic States.

Statistics for density of population are taken from the *World Almanac, 1933*, p. 327.

to be noted in most cases the existence of large cities. Seven of the ten largest American cities are located in the East and North. Is urban location a determinant in the formation of inter-institutional agreements? Table X shows the number of agreements formed by higher institutions located in the metropolitan areas of the ten biggest cities. These sixty-four agreements constitute 55 per cent of all agreements listed. Twenty-five additional agreements have been entered into by institutions, one of which is located in a city of 200,000 inhabitants or more. Urban location appears to be favorable to the formation of agreements.

TABLE X

NUMBER OF AGREEMENTS PARTICIPATED IN BY HIGHER INSTITUTIONS
IN 10 BIGGEST CITIES OF THE UNITED STATES

City	Population	Number of Agreements
New York	7,986,386	21
Chicago	4,364,755	6
Philadelphia	2,847,148	8
Los Angeles	2,318,526	2
Boston	2,307,897	14
Detroit	2,104,764	0
Pittsburgh	1,953,668	1
St. Louis	1,293,516	3
San Francisco	1,290,094	3
Cleveland	1,039,826	6
Total number of agreements		64

Population statistics taken from the *World Almanac, 1933,* pp. 344–45.

In the urban region not only is there greater density of population but there are larger numbers of higher institutions. These have greater opportunities for carrying out varied programs, inasmuch as there are opportunities for research provided by libraries, hospitals, museums, and botanical gardens. Transportation between these institutions is easier and less expensive than between institutions elsewhere. Finally, these institutions serve to a greater degree the same constituency and it seems only natural that the opportunities should be coordinated just as opportunities afforded by other social agencies are being coordinated. It will be remembered that there was mentioned (on page 3) the prediction of President Butler regarding the development of large "federated" universities in certain urban areas. The development of more closely knit social structure and the development of social planning would seem to indicate that more and more agreements will be formed in such regions.

TRANSPORTATION FACILITIES

Easy and inexpensive transportation facilities enable students and professors to pass from one institution to another, taking part in the programs of both. Facilities for transportation, as they are extended, will probably decrease the need for proximity between institutions taking part in agreements. Transportation facilities are already changing the local character of the college. Students are drawn from increased distances. As students from one area have greater and greater opportunities to attend different institutions, the constituencies of these different institutions will become more nearly the same. In consequence, the necessity will become more and more apparent for coordinating institutional programs and resources. The trend toward a greater range of service for the individual institution is indicated in the following citation:

Without question the tendency will be toward broadening the patronage field of schools. The real college field should be measured in transportation rather than miles. For years some schools have been able to draw students many miles along railroads and few miles at right angles to transportation. The advent of good roads, autos, bus connections, is breaking down isolation even in the mountains. The psychological isolation due to state lines is slightly diminishing. It is as easy for a student to go two hundred miles to college in this generation as it was to go fifty miles in the last generation. The Church will do well to broaden its horizon with regard to this aspect of education. Undoubtedly the time will come when a student may go from Texas to Virginia or from Virginia to Texas to secure the type of training he desires.[9]

In one instance, institutions under agreement were found to be providing their own transportation facilities. Furman University and Greenville Woman's College have agreed that both institutions shall share equally the expense involved in transporting students and faculty members to meet classes. As transportation facilities are developed the opportunities for interchange will become more and more apparent.

[9] Brown, B. W., *Report of the Survey of the Educational Work and Responsibility of the Presbyterian Church in the United States*, p. 19. Louisville, 1928.

PROSPECT OF FINANCIAL SAVING

The desire for economy in higher education is fostering the development of agreements. This is of particular influence at the present time in the face of the financial depression. Educators are viewing coordination as a means of meeting possible reductions in income.[10] The question has been raised whether there are too many separately conducted higher institutions, each necessitating elaborate investment and each striving to secure greater and greater resources.[11] Individual institutional development in higher education has led to duplication of offerings and often to open competition between neighboring institutions. In some cases, the standing of institutions has been judged by the number of courses they give and the number of professional schools they include, irrespective of the quality of the work done. Coordination of programs and resources is particularly desirable in the case of more specialized fields of knowledge. Such coordination is "economical financially and economical educationally. In all respects it illustrates sound educational ethics."[12] The resources resulting from such cooperation are increased for each institution. The grouping together of several colleges on a voluntary basis or the founding of new colleges in close association with existing institutions leads to economy in their conduct, more ample facilities than one could afford alone, and enlarged opportunities for staff and students.[13]

PROSPECT OF GREATER INSTITUTIONAL RECOGNITION

Agreements in some cases lead to greater institutional recognition and this motive appears undoubtedly to have played a part in their formation. Particularly is this the case where a small college becomes allied to a great university. The degree of the small college is endorsed or reënacted by the university; the name of the university is added to the corporate title of the college; and the faculty of the college receive university appointment. This sponsorship of

---

[10] Capen, S. P., "An Incomparable Challenge." *The Journal of Higher Education,* Vol. IV, No. 3, p. 110, March 1933.

[11] Jones, M. M., "College Financing." *Bulletin of the Association of American Colleges,* Vol. XVIII, No. 3, p. 352, November 1932.

[12] Butler, Nicholas Murray, *Annual Report.* Columbia University, 1906.

[13] An unpublished paper made available through the kindness of President J. A. Blaisdell, Claremont Colleges.

the small college by the university is recognized by other higher educational institutions and the students and faculty of the small college profit in consequence. In some cases the formation of an agreement with a neighboring university has led to the accreditation of the college by the regional association. This occurred in the case of the Corporate Colleges of St. Louis University.

At the meeting of the North Central Association of Colleges and Secondary Schools, March 18-20, 1926, it was voted to approve the plan of merging the nine Catholic Colleges in and near St. Louis with St. Louis University under the name of the "Corporate Colleges of St. Louis University" and to inspect these institutions in 1928 after the merger had been in operation two years. (*North Central Association Quarterly,* Vol. I, p. 18, June 1927.)

At the meeting of the North Central Association of Colleges and Secondary Schools held in Chicago in March, 1928, as a result of the final inspection of the Corporate Colleges of St. Louis University prescribed in the above paragraph, it was announced that "The Corporate Colleges of St. Louis University had been placed on the approved list" as members of the North Central Association of Colleges and Secondary Schools.[14]

PROSPECT OF GREATER SERVICE TO THE AREA

Institutions with broad vision have seen in the inter-institutional agreement an opportunity to unite all the agencies for higher education within the area behind a program of greater service. This motive, as was seen on page 6, led to the founding of the Cleveland Conference for Educational Cooperation, and to the agreement which will soon be put in force between the Case School of Applied Science and Western Reserve University. The same motive has played its part in many other agreements where institutions recognize the need for more effective service than is now provided and where there is need for the development of new lines of training. Although institutional advantage will and must continue to determine the development of separate institutions, the opportunities for increased service through cooperation will, it appears certain, influence this development to a greater and greater degree.

SUMMARY

In a very large proportion of the cases agreements have been consummated by institutions whose programs supplement each other, thereby affording greater opportunities than where separately

---

[14] *Bulletin of St. Louis University,* Catalog Number, Vol. XVII, No. 2, February 1931.

provided. Institutions whose programs are identical in most cases do not form agreements, or if they do, this is done with the object of developing differentiated programs emphasizing training which each is peculiarly fitted to give. Agreements are dependent to a considerable degree on the type of institution participating, certain types finding greater need of agreements than others. Size of college or university is not as much a determinant of agreements as is program. In future, perhaps the small college will form agreements to a much larger extent than at present.

Proximity is and has been an influential determinant of agreements, but this condition will undoubtedly change with the development of increased facilities for transportation. Agreements may be expected to develop in greatest numbers in urban locations where there are likely to be found many higher institutions, closer proximity, and more effective transportation facilities.

Minor motives in the formation of agreements to date have been the prospect of financial saving; greater institutional recognition; and greater service to the area. These play a part frequently in conjunction with each other and with the desire for more adequate institutional provision. In future, it appears evident that they will be more significant factors.

CHAPTER V

Changes in Structure and Function Resulting from Agreement

INTER-INSTITUTIONAL agreements show changes in institutional structure and function in the following fields: control; administration; faculty; and facilities. These changes are outlined in the present chapter, there being pointed out, wherever possible, the causes for the establishment of particular structure and function and the advantages inherent in them.

CONTROL

Institutions may coordinate their control through the interlocking directorate; the office of the chief executive officer; the advisory committee; election to the board of one institution or the other; conferment of all degrees under the authority of one institution or the other; endorsement of the degrees of one by the other.

The Interlocking Directorate

Two forms of structure have been found: the first provides that all members of one board of trustees be elected from the membership of the other; the second provides that a portion of the membership of each board serve on the other but that the remaining membership be separate and distinct. Where all trustees of one board are elected from the other, there is established high centralization of control resembling closely integral organization. Under the second form, where part of the membership of each board has no connection with the other, the two institutions draw on a more extensive field of support and on a wider range of interest than otherwise would be the case. The association between them is thus more flexible, depending upon the number of trustees elected in common and the desire of the participating institutions.

The first form of interlocking directorate has been utilized in the agreement between the Catholic Sisters' College and the Catholic University of America. The Catholic Sisters' College was founded by the University to carry on the undergraduate instruction of women, the desire being to avoid coeducation on the undergraduate level. The College thus carries on a portion of the total program of the University. The second form of interlocking directorate has been utilized both in the founding of new institutions and in the integration of existing institutions into a common educational system. It encourages cooperation between hitherto independent institutions by enabling friends of each to retain voice in that institution's management while bringing it into harmony with other institutions performing a somewhat similar program. Both forms of interlocking directorate insure separate legal identity for each institution and independent institutional responsibility for property and finances.

Examples of the second form of interlocking directorate are found in the following cases: When Western Reserve University was founded, provision was made that the University and Adelbert College have a majority of trustees in common. Later, new schools were founded under the University Board but there were also included through the interlocking directorate Cleveland College and the Cleveland School of Architecture. The University Board of Union University was created through the same structure. It is composed of the permanent trustees of Union College and representatives of the Albany Law School, the Albany Medical School, and the Albany College of Pharmacy. The University Foundation set up in Atlanta coordinated the control of Atlanta University, Morehouse College, and Spelman College through the same means. The interlocking directorate was employed to coordinate the control of Pomona College with that of the two new institutions: Claremont Colleges and Scripps College. When the Thomas W. Evans Museum and Dental Institute was founded, provision was made that its directorate be interlocking with that of the University of Pennsylvania. Cleveland College, which later was included in the system of Western Reserve University, has as members of its directorate since founding trustees of the Case School of Applied Science and of Western Reserve University.

Although the interlocking directorate has been employed to a considerable extent in industry, it has not been found in general use among institutions of higher learning. Some believe, however, that it is an especially favorable instrument for university organization. The decentralization which is thereby made possible enables a professional school to retain contact through its board of control with members of the profession, enlisting both their direction and their support. Thus, Bosworth and Jones commend the plan under which Western Reserve University is organized:

> This university is, as a whole, a refreshing exception in American institutions of higher learning. Its organization is based on administrative decentralization. It is a confederation of affiliated schools, each one of which has kept its own identity and autonomy within the university scheme. Its school of architecture is the Cleveland School of Architecture, originally organized and still partially supported by the Cleveland Chapter of A.I.A.[1]

The Chief Executive Officer

Coordination through this means is in reality a loose form of interlocking directorate. The president of one institution is elected ex-officio a member of the board of the allied institution. Thus, through his connection with his own board of trustees and that of the allied institution, coordination of control is brought about. Two forms of this structure were found: In one, the allied institutions elect the same president and he is elected ex-officio a member of the board of each. In the other, each institution has its own president but the president of one institution is elected ex-officio a member of the board of the other. The first practice, providing as it does for integral administrative organization, is followed by Columbia University in its agreements with Barnard College, the New York Post-Graduate Medical School and Hospital, and St. Stephen's College; and by the University of Southern California in its agreements with the College of Dentistry and the Los Angeles University of International Relations. The President of Columbia University is also a member of the Board of Teachers College, although no provision was found in the agreement that this should be the case. The second practice is found in the agreements with Atlanta University. The President of Atlanta University is ex-officio a member of the Boards of Morehouse and Spelman, although each of these colleges has its own president. It is also followed in the agreement between Vassar College and Sarah Lawrence College where the president of the former serves on the board of the latter.

This form of coordination of control is closely similar to a type

[1] Bosworth, F. H., Jr., and Jones, R. C., *A Study of Architectural Schools for the Association of Collegiate Schools of Architecture*, pp. 133-34. Charles Scribner's Sons, New York, 1932.

of coordination of administration. It enables the formation of a large number of agreements without altering to any considerable extent the composition of the boards of the participating institutions. At the same time, however, it does provide for harmonization of control. In the Atlanta University agreements it is linked with the interlocking directorate, whereas in the Columbia University agreements with five institutions it is linked with other forms of coordination of administration.

The Advisory Committee

Coordination of control may be effected through an advisory committee. Three agreements provide for coordination through this means, all of them participated in by schools of music or art. Closely similar to coordination through the interlocking directorate, the advisory committee does not require any changes in the composition of the existing boards. Coordination through the advisory committee has been worked out in three ways: On the Advisory Council of the Illinois Conservatory of Music there sit three representatives of the Trustees of MacMurray College; two representatives of the Trustees of Illinois College; and the Presidents of both institutions. Colorado College and Broadmoor Art Academy provide for an advisory committee of six members, three from each board of control. On the Advisory Board of the Pittsburgh Musical Institute, Inc., are two representatives of the University of Pittsburgh.

Election to the Board of One of the Participating Institutions

Coordination of control may be effected through the method of election employed in making up the board of control of one institution or the other. Three agreements provide for this practice. Two of these agreements have been entered into by schools of religion allied to state universities. These schools of religion have for their aim the fostering of religious interest on the university campus and differ in this respect from the primary aim of the theological seminary. The methods employed in bringing about coordination through this means are as follows: The Trustees of the School of Religion at the University of Iowa are nominated by nine church electors and by six electors of the University. The Trustees of the Montana School of Religion are elected by the religious bodies which have fifty or more students in the State University. They are elected in direct proportion to the representation of the denominations in the student body. The third agreement is between Harvard University and Radcliffe College and provides that three members of the Faculties of Harvard University, when elected, shall be chosen Trustees of Radcliffe.

Conferring All Degrees under the Authority of One Institution

Coordination of control through this practice has been followed where a college or professional school has entered into an agreement with a university, the agreement being of a high degree of intimacy. The students of the college receive their degrees from the university. The programs of the two institutions are recognized as being of the same standing and the diplomas which the students receive are the same as all other university diplomas. They bear the signature of the president of the university and also the signature of the dean of the college where the student is primarily enrolled.

Where this practice is followed, students may pursue all their work in the allied college or they may pursue the major portion of it there and take courses in the other schools of the university. The students of Catholic Sisters' College and St. Stephen's College take their entire programs in these institutions. Barnard College students may take courses at Teachers College but otherwise carry on all their work in Barnard. Other institutions whose degrees are granted by an allied institution but whose students study in the college and in the university as well are: California College of Pharmacy, Hastings College of the Law, and San Francisco Institute of Art, whose degrees are conferred by the University of California; the College of Pharmacy of the City of New York, the New York Post-Graduate Medical School and Hospital, and Teachers College, whose degrees are conferred by Columbia University; the College of Dentistry and the Los Angeles University of International Relations, whose degrees are conferred by the University of Southern California; the Cleveland School of Architecture, whose degrees are conferred by Western Reserve University.

By this practice the college or professional school waives the right to grant degrees as long as the agreement remains in force. The waiving of this right, however, is not considered a surrender of any powers granted under its charter. The board of trustees which grants the degree reserves the right to refuse its degree for cause to candidates of the allied institution. This is the same practice as is followed regarding candidates from other schools within the university.

Endorsement of Degrees Granted to Graduates of the Allied Institution

In two cases, where degrees are granted separately, the degrees of the allied colleges and their programs are vouched for by the university, and in recognition of this fact the university endorses the degree which the colleges confer. This practice is followed in the agreement between Radcliffe College and Harvard University. Thus, Radcliffe College may not confer its degree except with the approval of the President and Fellows of Harvard College. The Radcliffe diploma bears the endorsement of Harvard University in recognition of this fact. The diplomas granted by the colleges which have formed agreements with St. Louis University also bear the endorsement of the allied university. On them it is stated that the diploma is conferred by a particular corporate college of St. Louis University. In order that these degrees and programs may be of the required standing, the agreements provide that a representative of the University be present at all meetings of a particular college where a vote is taken on the awarding of degrees, and that he have veto power.

ADMINISTRATION

Institutions may coordinate their administration through: election of the same administrative officers; approval of appointments to an allied institution; an administrative board or council; supervision of the allied institution in case of need; informal counsel through administrative officers.

Election of the Same Administrative Officers

In some agreements provision is made that the same executive officers be elected, whereas in others it is provided that certain other administrative officers serve both institutions. The former practice is followed by Western Reserve University in its agreements with Adelbert College, Cleveland College, and the Cleveland School of Architecture; by Columbia University in its agreements with Barnard College, the College of Pharmacy, the New York Post-Graduate Medical School and Hospital, St. Stephen's College, and Teachers College; by Lawrence College in its agreement with the Institute of Paper Chemistry; and by the University of Southern California in its agreements with the College of Dentistry and the Los Angeles University of International Relations. The latter practice is followed by Columbia University in its agreement with the College of Pharmacy, where the Superintendent of Buildings and Grounds, the Librarian, and the Registrar of Columbia are officers of the College of Pharmacy; by Claremont Colleges, where its Controller serves also Pomona and Scripps.

Approval of Appointments to an Allied Institution

Coordination of administration may be effected through provision that the members of the staff of one institution be appointed only with the approval of the members of the other. Approval of appointments may require that the allied institution be consulted. This practice is followed in the agreements with Atlanta University, by which the Presidents of Morehouse and Spelman Colleges may be elected only after consultation with the President of Atlanta University. In the agreements where the president of a university has been elected president of the allied college, as in the case of the Columbia agreements, the trustees of the allied college elect the dean of that college upon the approval of the president of the university. Some agreements provide that all appointments to the staff must be approved by the allied institution, as in the case of the School of Religion at the University of Iowa; or must be nominated by the trustees of the allied institution, as in the case of the Otho S. A. Sprague Memorial Institute; or must be elected by the concurrent action of the two boards, as in the case of the Thomas W. Evans Museum and Dental Institute.

An Administrative Board or Council

Coordination of administration may be effected through some administrative body on which sit representatives of the participating institutions. These administrative bodies differ in their composition and function.

The administrative Board of the Corporate Colleges of St. Louis University was instituted with the aim of coordinating the administration of the allied colleges under the leadership of the University. Through this board, the University lends assistance to the colleges by provision for the interchange of staff members with the University; recognition of standardized courses in the colleges; endorsement of the degrees granted by the colleges; appointment to the university staff of faculty members of the colleges who are of university standard; extension of university privileges to the faculty of the colleges; and promotion of educational development of these institutions in other ways. The Board is composed of the Most Reverend Archbishop of St. Louis, or his representative; the President of the University, or his representative; and two representatives from each of the colleges, one to represent the administrative function and the other the educational function of each institution. Representation of these two functions is found in the organization of several administrative boards which have been established. In some agreements, representation occurs in two different boards, one of the administrative board and the other the instructional board, or general faculty.

The Columbia University Council is another type of administrative board. Its function has been to coordinate the administration of the various schools of the University. Representation on it has been granted not only to those schools which are integrally organized under the University Board but also to certain other schools with which the University has formed agreements. As Monroe Smith points out, the Columbia University Council has been an instrument of great importance to the University in the formation of agreements.[2] It has enabled the University to coordinate the administration of institutions which have been brought into its educational system from time to time and it has permitted different degrees of intimacy with these institutions, depending on their type, standing, and the association desired. The intimacy of association has been determined by representation on the Council. Thus, through agreement Barnard College, the College of Pharmacy, the New York Post-Graduate Medical School and Hospital, St. Stephen's College, and Teachers College have been granted representation by their deans with full power to vote on all questions. They have also been granted an additional representative with similar powers, when their faculties comprise ten or more professors. These additional representatives are elected by the respective faculties, and in this way provision is made for representation of both their administrative and their educational functions. Two other institutions are represented upon the Council: Union The-

[2] *History of Columbia University, 1754-1904*, p. 252. Columbia University Press, New York, 1905.

ological Seminary and the General Theological Seminary. These are entitled to only one representative, who has the privilege of the floor without right to vote. The other seminaries allied to Columbia are granted no representation on the University Council.

Under agreement with the University of California the Dean of Hastings College of the Law was granted a seat in the University Senate during his lifetime with full right to vote.

At Claremont Colleges there are an Administrative Council and an Educational Council. These act to coordinate the administration of the three institutions associated at Claremont. The Educational Council is elected by the General Faculty. The Administrative Council is made up of the presidents of the three institutions, one representative from each college, and the controller of the three institutions. This Council coordinates also the administration of Claremont Colleges and La Verne College. The President and one representative of La Verne are granted access to the Council on all matters affecting the agreement between the two institutions.

The two administrative committees of Radcliffe College are the Council and the Academic Board. Coordination of its administration with Harvard University is achieved through representation on these bodies by members of the Faculty of Arts and Sciences of the University, these representatives being also teachers or trustees of Radcliffe. The Council directs the educational work, government of students, conferment of degrees, and expenditures of the College. The Academic Board, subject to the Council, directs instruction, examinations, and recommendation of candidates for degrees.

Another administrative body is the Administrative Board on Post-Graduate Studies in Medicine established by Columbia University in its agreement with the New York Post-Graduate Medical School and Hospital. The latter institution is represented on this board, although it is also represented on the University Council. This board, subject to University Statutes, has oversight and control over all post-graduate studies in medicine carried on in any part of the University.

Supervision of One Institution by the Other during Emergency

In one agreement there was found the provision that one institution delegate its powers to the other in case of emergency. This stipulation states that Radcliffe College may confer at any time upon the President and Fellows of Harvard College such powers of visitation and of direction and control over its management as the said Radcliffe College may deem it wise to confer, and the said President and Fellows of Harvard College may consent to assume.[3]

Informal Discussion and Contact between Officers of Allied Institutions

All agreements have the general provision, implicit or explicit, that administrative officers of allied institutions may confer on all matters where the problems of coordination make such conference desirable.

FACULTY

Coordination of the teaching staff of allied institutions may be effected through: the method employed in making appointments; representation of one institution upon the faculty of the other; provision for faculty standing in allied institutions; interchange of staff members between institutions.

Faculty Appointments

Several methods have been employed by allied institutions in making appointments. Appointment may require the joint action or approval of the allied institutions. In the agreement between the University of Pennsylvania and the Thomas W. Evans Museum and Dental Institute concurrent action is required for appointments to their joint program. Similar practice is followed by Simmons College and the Lowthorpe School of Landscape Architecture in making appointments for their combination course. Where two institutions have the same president the method followed is that of integral administrative organization. A faculty member is nominated for appointment by the dean of the allied college to its trustees, but appointment requires the approval of the two institutions. Faculty members are in some cases nominated by the administrative officer of the allied institution for appointment to the trustees of the other institution. This practice is followed in the case of the colleges allied to the University of California. It is also followed by the National Academy of Design in the case of instructors who are to give courses in fine arts at New York University. Faculty members may be nominated also to the staff of the allied institu-

[3] *Official Register of Harvard University*, Catalogue Issue, Vol. XXVIII, No. 46, p. 671, November 1931.

tion by the trustees of the other. This method is followed by the University of Chicago in appointment of faculty members to the staff of the Otho S. A. Sprague Memorial Institute. Another method requires that faculty appointment to the staff of the allied institutions be made only after consultation with the president of the other institution. Thus, faculty appointments to Morehouse and Spelman Colleges require that the presidents of these institutions consult with the President of Atlanta University.

Representation on the Faculty of One Institution by Members of an Allied Institution

Representation by Administrative Officers. The administrative officer of one institution is made in some cases ex-officio a member of the faculty of the other. This may occur under integral administrative organization, as when the President of Columbia University presides at the meetings of the Faculties of Barnard, the College of Pharmacy, the New York Post-Graduate Medical School and Hospital, St. Stephen's College, and Teachers College. It may also occur when the chief executive officers of the two institutions are different. Thus, the President of the University of California is president of the faculties of the allied colleges. The dean of each of the three colleges is also ex-officio a member of the Faculty of the University of California, designated as such by the directors of his college.

Representation by Faculty Members Ex-Officiis. Representation on the faculty of one institution may occur through appointment ex-officiis of members of the faculty of the other. Thus, representatives of the Columbia University Departments of Botany, Chemistry, Physiological Chemistry, and Materia Medica, when designated by the President of the University, are members ex-officiis of the Faculty of the College of Pharmacy. University professors of education, philosophy, and psychology are members ex-officiis of the Faculty of Teachers College, and the professor of mechanical engineering is a member of this faculty as long as his students use the Teachers College workshops. Ex-officio appointment is also given by the agreement with the University of Chicago to the members of the staff of the Otho S. A. Sprague Memorial Institute. The Director and members of the staff of the Institute are appointed members of the appropriate faculties of the University.

Representation by Special Appointment. Coordination of the teaching staffs of the two institutions may be accomplished through special representation on the faculty of one institution by members of the faculty of the other. The Faculties of Philosophy and Political Science of Columbia University nominate annually to the Trustees of the University for appointment to seats on these faculties two members each of the Faculty of Union Theological Seminary. Another example occurred in the case of the agreement with the New York School of Social Work. Columbia University established a professorship of applied sociology, the incumbent of which was to be the representative of the New York School of Social Work in the Columbia University faculties. By the same agreement there was constituted a faculty for the New York School of Social Work to which there were appointed, among others, three officers of Columbia University, nominated by the President of the University. The Director of the Perkins Observatory of Ohio Wesleyan University by the agreement with Ohio State University is appointed a non-resident lecturer in the latter. The Director of the School of American Research is head of the Departments of Anthropology and Archeology at the University of New Mexico.

Representation in a Common Faculty for the Allied Institutions. In some cases, a common faculty is instituted for the participating institutions. An example of this practice occurs in the agreements entered into by the colleges associated at Claremont. All professors and associate professors of Pomona and Scripps Colleges and faculty appointees of Claremont Colleges are members of the General Faculty.

Faculty Standing

Coordination of the teaching staffs of allied institutions may be accomplished through provision that the faculty members of each institution be accorded the same standing. Thus, it is provided that the faculty members of Barnard College be assured the same standing as those of corresponding rank in Columbia University. The general provision is made that faculty members of Barnard, the College of Pharmacy, the New York Post-Graduate Medical School and Hospital, St. Stephen's College, and Teachers College be faculty members of the University. The names of the faculty of the Berkeley Divinity School are included in the list of the General Faculty of Yale University and to them are accorded the privileges of the University on the same basis as such are accorded to the faculty members of the Yale Divinity School. The staffs of Broadmoor Art Academy and Colorado College through agreement are placed on a parity with each other.

Contrary to this practice is the practice, stipulated in certain agreements, which provides that equal standing be granted only to certain members of the allied institution. Thus, the names of the faculty members of the seminaries allied to the University of Chicago are listed separately in the University Register under the title, "Faculties of Affiliated Theological Seminaries," and an individual member of such a faculty becomes a member of the Faculty of the University only when so appointed. Appointment to the staff of St. Louis University occurs only when members of the faculties of the Corporate Colleges of St. Louis University conform to the standards of the University.

Interchange of Staff

Coordination of the teaching staffs of two institutions may be accomplished through members of one teaching in the other institution. In only a few agreements examined were there specific references to this practice. Provision is made in the agreement with Catholic Sisters' College that all instruction in this institution be carried on by the staff of the Catholic University of America. Many Columbia University teachers give instruction in Barnard College. The practice followed is for the Dean of Barnard to submit annually a statement to the President of Columbia University specifying the faculty needs of the College for the ensuing year. In this statement there is given the number and rank of officers of instruction and the amount of service desired in each subject. Certain teachers of Harvard University give instruction in Radcliffe College. The Case School of Applied Science annually conducts courses in Cleveland College in astronomy, mathematics, physics, engineering, and industrial technology. The University of Cincinnati gives courses in Comparative Religions open to students of Hebrew Union College annually, in exchange for which a faculty member of the College gives a course at the University in alternate years in the Literary History of the Bible. An arrangement exists whereby faculty members of the University of Denver are given special appointments to teach in the Iliff School of Theology, and faculty members of the School of Theology are given appointments to teach in the University. Prior to the agreement which has just been put in force, a professor of Claremont Colleges lectured in elementary education at La Verne College, whereas a professor of La Verne College conducted a seminar in comparative education at Claremont Colleges.[4] Whether this arrangement has been continued is not evident, but it seems probable that the new agreement provides for greater interchange of faculty than heretofore.

Interchange of faculty undoubtedly occurs to a much greater extent than would appear from the few examples given. It will be remembered that one function of the Administrative Board of the Corporate Colleges of St. Louis University is to arrange for interchange of staff members. In the agreements entered into by the University of Southern California the very general provision occurs that the same interrelationship shall take place between the staffs of the allied institutions as between the staffs of the other schools within the University.

Remuneration of staff members dividing their time between allied institutions may be provided for in two ways: Under the first method each institution pays the staff member directly for the hours of service he devotes to its program. Such is the arrangement which has been worked out by the University of Denver and the Iliff School of Theology. Under the second method the full salary of the staff member is paid by the institution where he is primarily employed and compensation for his service is then made to that institution by the other for the service he renders it. This compensation may be either a monetary return or an exchange of service whereby each institution carries on instruction or other services for the other. Under this second method, the arrangement is kept between the two institutions. This has the advantage that the institution in which a staff member gives his principal service determines his entire load. The needs of this institution come first and all arrangements for division of service have the approval of its chief executive officer. Interchange of staff, as pointed out by the Cleveland Conference for Educational Cooperation, is carried on for the purpose of improving educational opportunities, for the improvement of the effectiveness of the staff member, and for the purpose of additional remuneration to the staff member.[5] The

[4] A new agreement was reported by President James A. Blaisdell of Claremont Colleges between La Verne College and that institution in the following article: "Claremont Colleges—Enlarging Plans." *Bulletin of the Association of American Colleges*, Vol. XIX, No. 2, pp. 187-90, May 1933.

[5] *The Cleveland Conference for Educational Cooperation, Annual Reports and*

last of these purposes is the least desirable. Sufficient remuneration should be paid by the institution in which the staff member is primarily employed in order that other remuneration be not necessary. All division of services between two institutions should form part of the accepted load of the staff member in the institution in which he gives principal service. Only in cases of necessity and then only for a brief period should such services in the allied institution be in the nature of over-time service.

FACILITIES

Institutions may coordinate their facilities through: opening courses of one institution to members of the other; development of a combined course leading to a degree from one institution or the other; extension of the general privileges of one institution to members of the other; extension of specific privileges of one institution to the other.

Opening Courses of One Institution to Members of the Other

Provision for this practice is found in almost all agreements, exceptions occurring in the following: where agreements are solely for the purpose of interchange of staff members or research facilities; where allied institutions are located at considerable distance from each other; where the agreement provides for coordination or administration without interchange of courses; where agreements are between men's and women's institutions and coeducation is thought undesirable on the undergraduate level. Interchange of courses is governed by regulations as to eligibility, recognition of credits, and charges for tuition.

Eligibility. Institutions differ widely as to the conditions under which students of one institution may enroll in the courses of the other. Where a close agreement has been established all courses are generally thrown open to all qualified students of both institutions, subject to the general administrative regulations of both institutions. Under agreements of less intimacy, specific regulations are to be found which differ from institution to institution. These prescribe the kind of student who is eligible and the kind of courses for which he may enroll.

Some of the qualifications set upon the eligibility of the student

---

Committee Reports, pp. 28-30. The Cleveland Conference for Educational Cooperation, Euclid Avenue, Cleveland, Ohio, 1928.

are as follows: He must be a regular member of one institution or the other; he must be recommended by the department head or dean of the institution in which he is primarily enrolled; he must receive the approval of the dean or president of the institution in which he wishes to enroll; he must receive the approval of the instructor of the course in which he wishes to enroll; he must have studied in the institution where he is primarily enrolled for a specified period of time; and he must have achieved a certain scholastic rank there. Furthermore, no student to whom admission had been refused to either institution may be granted admission to it by virtue of its agreement with the other.

Some of the qualifications set upon the courses for which a student may enroll are as follows: they must fulfill part of the requirements toward his degree; they must be so designated by the two institutions; they must be given in certain departments or schools of the allied institution; they must be courses which are not found in the institution in which the student is primarily enrolled. In addition, there must be sufficient enrollment in the course by students of the institution which gives it in order that the institution be not compelled to give a course for the sake alone of the students of the other.

Credit. Agreements provide differently for the amount of credit granted work in allied institutions. In some cases, credit is granted for such work on the same basis as for work in the institution in which the student is primarily enrolled. The determination of these credits is based on degree requirements. In other cases, limitations are placed on the amount of credit to be obtained from courses in the allied institution. The courses for which credit is given are frequently specified. They also are frequently subject to the approval of a curriculum committee or an administrative officer in the institution granting the degree. Frequently also, where they are subject to approval, they are subject to evaluation, greater or less credit being given for work in the allied institution. The number of points for which credit is given is frequently specified.

Charges for Tuition. Courses in one allied institution may be opened, with or without charges, to students of the other.

a) Remission of Charges. Provision is found in a large number of agreements that the courses of one institution, under specific regulation as to eligibility, be opened to members of the other without charge. With two exceptions these agreements have been formed between theological seminaries and other institutions. Remission of charges to students of theological schools appears to have resulted from the tendency to provide training to theological students at as little cost as possible. Colleges and universities have cooperated with institutions giving training for the ministry by placing their educational resources at the disposal of these institutions (see page 33). This cooperation appears to be based on the assumption that the number of students availing themselves of these privileges will be small and that the increased expense will be negligible. The restrictions as to eligibility, both in regard to type of student and kind of course, emphasize the fact that the numbers are to be kept small—in some agreements limited to men of high rank and to enrollment in but two courses without charge. One agreement specifically states that should the agreement lead to undue expense to either institution, it may be later modified and tuition charged, the total tuition charged any student, however, being no greater than that for a full program at his own institution. The courses of Columbia University and Union Theological Seminary were formerly opened to students of the other without charge, but later this arrangement was modified to the effect that students of each institution must pay for courses in the other at the current charge and must also pay administration fees. Another university reported that the plan of opening its courses without charge to students of allied seminaries was now under consideration and might soon be modified.

Agreements with theological schools which provide for free tuition are as follows: Courses are opened by: Boston University School of Theology to students of the Episcopal Theological School, the Harvard Divinity School, and Newton Theological Institution; Clark University, Georgia, to students of the Gammon Theological Seminary; Columbia University to students of Bloomfield Theological Seminary, Drew Theological Seminary, the General Theological Seminary, the Jewish Theological Seminary of America, St. Joseph's Theological Seminary, and the Theological Seminary of the Reformed Church in America; the Episcopal Theological Seminary to students of the Harvard Divinity School; the Harvard Divinity School and the Harvard Graduate Faculty of Arts and Sciences to students of Boston University School of Theology, the Crane Theological School, the Episcopal Theological School, and Newton

Theological Institution; Northwestern University to students of the Garrett Biblical Institute and Western Theological Seminary and these institutions opened their courses in return; the University of Pennsylvania to students of Crozer Seminary and the Episcopal Divinity School; Vanderbilt University to students of Scarritt College for Christian Workers and the Southern College of the Y. M. C. A.; George Peabody College for Teachers to the same institutions; and the Yale Divinity School to students of the Berkeley Divinity School and the Berkeley Divinity School in return to students of the Yale Divinity School.

The two agreements which have been formed by institutions other than theological schools and which remit tuition are as follows: The first is a very loose agreement between Harvard University and Massachusetts Institute of Technology, developed following the failure of the former agreement between these institutions. Both institutions open research and advanced courses, not part of an undergraduate program, to students of the other following the consent of the instructor or department head under which this work is taken. The other agreement is between Vanderbilt University and George Peabody College for Teachers. It provides that full-time students in either institution may enroll without charge for twelve hours in the other, subject to the approval of the Vanderbilt Committee on Affiliation. It is recommended that these twelve hours be divided between junior and senior years.

b) Charges for Tuition. Where charges are made for tuition, students of each institution pay at a rate agreed upon or at the current rate. Two practices have been followed in regard to the payment of tuition charges: Under the first, the student pays the allied institution for the courses he takes in it. This arrangement is thus between the student and the allied institution, subject to the advice of the student's counselor, of course, in the institution in which he is primarily enrolled. Under the second practice the student pays tuition for his entire program to the institution in which he is primarily enrolled and that institution remunerates the other for the total service rendered its students. The arrangement in this case is kept between the institutions and is more desirable in that the institutions can keep track of the total interchange which is taking place and can thereby coordinate their own work to a greater degree or develop new training to meet the demand for it.

Some agreements specify the exact amount one institution shall pay the other for each course or point pursued in the other. In general, however, some method of payment is agreed upon whereby the current charge for tuition is multiplied by the total number of hours for which the students of one institution register in the other. At the end of each academic period, each institution sends the other a statement of its students who have enrolled for work in the other and the total number of hours taken. On the basis of these two statements payment is made. Provision for payment at the current rate avoids the possibility that changes in tuition charge will necessitate in future the drawing up of a new contract. Certain of the Columbia University agreements have had to be modified in this respect.

Development of a Combined Course Leading to a Degree
from One Institution or the Other

Programs of allied institutions may be coordinated through a prescribed course of study, carried in part by each institution but leading to a degree from one. This practice differs from a mere opening of courses of one institution to students of the other in that it usually sets up a new degree program. In some instances the degree had been offered by neither institution prior to the agreement. In other cases, such as the agreement between the Yale Law School and the Harvard Graduate School of Business Administration, a new type of professional training has been developed, giving legal education with business training.

The combination course has been most frequently employed by schools of art or music. These have joined with schools of education in a university or with a college in setting up a degree course for teachers of art or music. The technical courses or applied work in such cases is offered by the school of art or music and the theoretical courses by the college or university.

Provision is made in some combination courses that the student enroll in both institutions at the same time. In other courses the student spends a year or more at each institution. The agreement with the Lowthorpe School of Landscape Architecture specifies that students spend their first two years at Simmons, their third year at Lowthorpe, and their final year at Simmons. The Harvard-Yale agreement provides that the student spend his first year at the Yale Law School, his second year at Harvard, and his final two years at Yale. The agreement between Teachers College, Columbia University, and the Teachers Institute of the Jewish Theological Seminary of America specifies that the student spend his first two years at the Institute, his second two years in a program of part-time teaching while pursuing work at the Institute or at other New York higher institutions, and his final year at Teachers College. This course is of interest because it involves two agreements: that between the Institute and Teachers College; and that between Teachers College and Columbia University which confers the degree.

Recommendation of candidates for a degree from a combination course may be made by the faculties of both institutions jointly, as in the agreement between the School of Education of the University of Pittsburgh and the Pittsburgh Musical Institute, Inc. On the other hand, candidates may be recommended by the faculty of the institution granting the degree, consideration being given by that faculty to the advice of the allied institution. The agreement entered into by the Cleveland Institute of Music states specifically that final judgment on requirements for the degree rests with the faculties of Western Reserve University.

Extension of the General Privileges of One Institution to the Other

Institutions have frequently made available to each other not only instruction but also land, buildings, equipment, and services of a non-instructional nature. This has meant in some cases simply the extension of certain college or university privileges to members of the allied institution. In other cases it has meant donation, loan, or lease of facilities. In still other instances, institutions own and administer jointly certain services, each institution defraying a portion of the cost. Below are presented instances of these forms of cooperation.

The extension of the general privileges of one institution to members of the other is stated in various ways. Thus, Teachers College is included in the educational system of Columbia University and enjoys the "privileges and obligations" of other schools within the University. Barnard College, the College of Pharmacy, the Post-Graduate Medical School and Hospital, and St. Stephen's enjoy the same privileges. The Bible College of Missouri enjoys the hospitality of the University of Missouri, and the libraries, museum, health service, and other privileges of the University are open to its students. Faculty members of the Berkeley Divinity School are accorded access to libraries, museums, and other resources of Yale University on the same basis as are faculty members of the Yale Divinity School. Students when duly certified by the Dean of the Berkeley Divinity School are afforded the privileges of the Yale Divinity School. The University of Pennsylvania opens all privileges enjoyed by other schools and departments of the University to the members of the Thomas W. Evans Museum and Dental Institute. St. Louis University "as far as possible" places its educational resources at the disposal of the corporate colleges. The agreement between the University of Southern California and the Los Angeles University of International Relations specifies that the libraries and other facilities of each institution be made available to the other. The officers and students of the allied seminaries of the University of Chicago are granted the privileges of the libraries, museums, and gymnasiums of the University and the members of the University are accorded the privileges of the libraries and museums of the seminaries.

Recognition that these privileges have been granted the allied institution and that the relationship established is extremely close is made, in some cases, by adding the name of the larger institution to the corporate title of the other. For instance, to the corporate title of Adelbert College, Cleveland College, and the Cleveland School of Architecture the words "of Western Reserve University" are added. Adelbert College and Cleveland College grant their own degrees, nevertheless, but the degrees for students of architecture are granted by Western Reserve University. Likewise, to the title of the College of Dentistry and to that of Los Angeles University of International Relations is added the title of the University of Southern California; to the title of Catholic Sisters' College is added that of the Catholic University of America; and to that of Teachers College is added the title of Columbia University. The title "School of Dentistry, University of Pennsylvania" is placed below the name "The Thomas W. Evans Museum and Dental Institute" on the building erected by the latter.

*Extension of Specific Privileges of One Institution
    to Members of the Other*

With respect to Campus and Land. The Bible College of Missouri is located on the campus of the University of Missouri. The

College of the Bible and Transylvania College are located on the same campus. The University of Chicago furnishes free of rent the land on which the Otho S. A. Sprague Memorial Institute is located. Garrett Biblical Institute leases its land from Northwestern University. Lawrence College donated the land on which is situated the Institute of Paper Chemistry, there being the understanding that this land shall revert to the College in case the Institute ceases to operate. When the Mary Reed Library was built by the University of Denver, the Iliff School of Theology donated approximately half an acre to the site. The library of the theological school is now housed in the Mary Reed Library. Witwatersrand University provided the land for the observatory established by Yale University, the land to revert to Witwatersrand at the discontinuance of the observatory.

With respect to Classroom Buildings. Provision was made in the agreement with Hastings College of the Law that the University of California set aside a room or suitable hall for the use of the College. In the agreement with the San Francisco Institute of Art it was provided that the Institute use such portions of the building donated by Edward F. Searles as necessary for its purposes and consistent with the use of the property by the University of California. Through agreement, a portion of Academy Hall was rented by Illinois College for the use of the Illinois Conservatory of Music. This building provides studios, practice rooms, and assembly hall. Witwatersrand University agreed to erect a building or buildings to serve the observatory established by Yale University and to include laboratory, offices, and living quarters for the astronomer in charge.

With respect to Dormitories. Students of the seminaries allied to the University of Chicago are permitted to occupy rooms in the dormitories of the University provided they are registered and matriculated in the Graduate Divinity School of the University. The College of the Bible owns jointly with Transylvania College its residence for men. The dormitories for women of Transylvania College are open to women students of the College of the Bible.

With respect to Libraries. The University of Chicago agrees to house, should they so desire, the libraries of the allied seminaries, provided there is space, without cost. The seminaries are held responsible for the maintenance and administration of these libraries. Claremont Colleges has established a library to serve the colleges associated at Claremont. Atlanta University has followed similar practice. The Columbia University agreements state that the students of the College of Pharmacy, the General Theological Seminary, St. Stephen's College, Teachers College, and Union Theological Seminary be accorded the same privileges as Columbia students in the use of the University library and that these institutions grant the same opportunities to Columbia students. Women students of Columbia University are granted the privileges of the Barnard College Library and Barnard students are accorded the privileges of the University Library. Through agreement the Librarian of Columbia was empowered to transfer to the Library of Union Theological Seminary such books on theology and ecclesiastical history as he may select, subject to the approval of the President of the University. Columbia has also transferred to Teachers College certain books dealing with education. In the agreement with Teachers College it is provided that the Teachers College Library be administered in cooperation with the general University library system. Vanderbilt University and George Peabody College for Teachers make their respective libraries available to students and teachers of the other on equal terms with members of their own institution.

With respect to Other Buildings. Claremont Colleges established an auditorium and certain other buildings to house services it provides for the associated colleges: health and infirmary service, the business office, and the summer session. The same administration building serves Atlanta University and Morehouse and Spelman Colleges.

With respect to Equipment. Few agreements provide specifically for coordination of equipment. Where such provision is made, the equipment is of a specialized character. Thus, through agreement, Illinois College sold its musical instruments and musical equipment to MacMurray College at the time that the Illinois Conservatory of Music was established. The Yerkes Observatory makes available to the Perkins Observatory a stellar spectrograph to be kept at the Perkins Observatory. The Perkins Observatory furnishes the use of a 69-inch reflector to the Yerkes Observatory during a portion of the night and agrees to keep the telescope in repair and to pay running expenses on it. The equipment of the observatory established by Yale University on the campus of Witwatersrand University remains the property of Yale University and may be removed by that University.

With respect to certain Non-Instructional Services. Certain services have been indicated in the discussion of buildings and equipment. Other instances should be noted. Northwestern University furnishes heat, light, and water to Garrett Biblical Institute at rates made available through its own plant. Illinois College furnishes heat, light, and janitor service to Academy Hall, a portion of which is utilized by the Illinois Conservatory of Music. Transylvania College and the College of the Bible own their own heating plant in common. Plant maintenance, heat, janitorial service, stores, and purchases in the allied colleges are under the control of Western Reserve University. The University of Pennsylvania makes its organization for publicity available to the Thomas W. Evans Museum and Dental Institute.

SUMMARY

Structure and function set up under agreement have been determined primarily by the desire to enlarge and make more adequate the offerings of respective institutions. Although the economy motive has played its part, modification of institutional structure for the sake of economy has followed the demand for greater provision.

Joint ownership of facilities or complete differentiation of offerings has had to wait, in general, on replacement by one institution or the other. Following the formation of an agreement, economy becomes to a greater and greater degree possible. Certain agreements between institutions show this trend toward unification of common services to an outstanding degree.

Agreements differ widely in the structure which they set up. In some cases institutional needs require practically no changes in structure or function. In other cases close association is demanded, and there is then brought about a coordination of administration and control that gives institutions almost the same relationship that would prevail if they were schools organized under a single board.

Where institutions have formed several agreements for accomplishing the same or similar purposes, the trend is for these to resemble each other. Evaluation of types of structure is not possible, however, without intensive study of institutional needs. A survey of each institution desiring to participate in an agreement is necessary to determine the structure and function to be set up. With more intensive study of institutional needs and structure the patterns for coordination will become more possible of evaluation.

CHAPTER VI

Institutional Identity and Powers under Agreement

COORDINATION has been prevented many times by the fear that participating institutions will thereby lose their identity or be deprived of rights and powers granted under their charters. In recognition of this danger, there have frequently been included in agreements special provisions for the safeguarding of powers and identity. Examination of these provisions is of importance to any project for coordinating the work of independent institutions. The special provisions to be discussed relate to: integrity of charters; identity and general powers of corporations; control of property and finances; control of programs; control of students; powers for modification and termination of agreements.

INTEGRITY OF CHARTERS

No modification of charters is necessitated by reason of participation in agreements. Inter-institutional agreements are consummated entirely under the authority of the institutions participating in them and require no new action or specific sanction by the legislature of the state or states in which the institutions are located.

This integrity of charters is specified in several agreements: The union between the Corporate Colleges and St. Louis University is declared to be of a non-legal character. Provision is made in the agreements with Atlanta University that the charter of this institution shall not be considered modified by these contracts with respect to either intent or purpose. There is to be no change in the name of either institution as a result of the agreement between the National Academy of Design and New York University. The Columbia University agreements with Barnard College, the College of Pharmacy, St. Stephen's College, and Teachers College state that the agreements with these institutions shall not be considered a surrender of powers conferred upon them by their charters. These institutions merely waive certain powers during the continuance of the agreement. Similar provision occurs in the agreement with

Los Angeles University of International Relations in regard to powers conferred upon it by its Articles of Incorporation.

IDENTITY AND GENERAL POWERS OF CORPORATIONS

Certain agreements specify that the identity and general powers of corporations shall not be affected by the terms of the contract which has been consummated. The agreement between Broadmoor Art Academy and Colorado College specifies that there shall be no corporate merger. The agreements between Cleveland College, the Cleveland School of Architecture, Adelbert College, and Western Reserve University state that the colleges shall continue their separate identity. The allied colleges of the University of California, it is specified in their agreements, shall not be deprived of their boards of trustees. There is to be no surrender of the powers with which these corporations have been vested. The National Academy of Design and New York University provide in their agreement that the control and management of the two institutions be separate and independent. The Columbia University agreements with Barnard College, the College of Pharmacy, St. Stephen's College, and Teachers College provide that each of the allied institutions retain all powers not delegated through agreement and that the delegation of powers shall not be a surrender of powers. Similar provision is made in the agreement between Los Angeles University of International Relations and the University of Southern California.

CONTROL OF PROPERTY AND FINANCE

Provision is likewise made that there shall continue to be separate control of property and finances following the formation of an agreement. Furthermore, it is provided that the financial standing of participating institutions is not to be endangered by the agreement. Each institution is to assume no liability for the past, present, or future debts of the other, and each is to support and maintain its own corporate organization and its own faculty.

Instances of these provisions are as follows: The agreements entered into by the allied colleges of the University of California state specifically that each institution is to retain full control of its property. It is also stated that the University is not liable for the acts or contracts of the colleges. The agreement with Catholic Sisters' College specifies that the College shall be responsible for its property and maintenance. The agreement between Colorado College and

Broadmoor Art Academy states that there shall be entirely separate control of property, the handling of endowment and income, the payment of faculty, and furthermore specifies that neither institution shall be liable for the obligations of the other. In the Columbia agreements, it is stated that Barnard College, the College of Pharmacy, the New York Post-Graduate Medical School and Hospital, St. Stephen's College, and Teachers College shall maintain and support their corporate organizations and that the University shall be liable for no other duties than those specified in the agreements. The freedom of the University from obligation, liability, or responsibility for maintenance, support, direction, and management of these institutions is emphasized. Provision is also made specifically that Barnard and St. Stephen's Colleges provide for, support, and maintain the members of their respective faculties. In the agreements with the University of Southern California, it is provided that the College of Dentistry and the Los Angeles University of International Relations support their own corporate organizations. In the agreements with the Corporate Colleges of St. Louis University it is stated that the University shall have no supervision, jurisdiction, or control over the finances of these institutions. Yale University is not to be responsible for the property or conduct of the Berkeley Divinity School. Adelbert College, Cleveland College, and the Cleveland School of Architecture, by agreement with Western Reserve University, retain complete control over their property and finances. On the other hand, it is indicated that aid to an allied college is sometimes given by a university under agreement by the fact that Western Reserve University has on certain occasions and by special vote of its corporation granted subventions for the support of its allied colleges.

CONTROL OF PROGRAM

Autonomy in regard to institutional program is preserved by special provisions in certain agreements relating to standing, preservation of quality of work in spite of changes which may occur in the management of the allied institution, and preservation of the distinctive character of each institution.

Instances of these special provisions are as follows: In the agreement between Broadmoor Art Academy and Colorado College provision is made that each institution shall select its own faculty and fix its own standards of admission and credits. In addition, each institution reserves the right to decide on tuition fees for its courses. Furthermore, although there is to be differentiation of program, each institution decides the extent to which it will provide courses in the entire field allotted to it. The College of Pharmacy and Teachers College, in their agreements with Columbia University, are insured the exercise of direction and control over all instruction which they give. The agreements between the allied colleges and the University of California provide that the colleges shall not be deprived of their faculties as a result of agreements contracted by them with the University. It is provided that the authority and autonomy of the Institute of Musical Art and Teachers College be preserved over their offerings of courses and over their granting of certificates, degrees, and diplomas.

Special provisions relate to the preservation of the distinctive character of participating institutions. The agreements with Atlanta University insure Morehouse and Spelman Colleges full control over such religious and moral instruction as each desires to give. The Columbia University agreement with St. Stephen's College provides that the religious policy of the College be under the control of its Board of Trustees, acting through its Warden, who shall be a communicant member of the Protestant Episcopal Church.

CONTROL OF STUDENTS

There are found in certain agreements provisions specifying which institution shall exercise care and control of students. Greenville Woman's College continues full control and discipline over its students attending classes in Furman University. Furman authorities, on the other hand, may report improper and unsatisfactory conduct and finally exclude unsatisfactory students from its campus and classrooms. The Institute of Musical Art and Teachers College reserve in their agreement full control over their students. The agreement between Columbia University and St. Stephen's College specifies that the athletic policy of the College be under the control of the Trustees of St. Stephen's. The group of colleges at Claremont through their agreements emphasize the integrity and esprit de corps of their separate student bodies.

POWERS FOR MODIFICATION AND TERMINATION OF AGREEMENTS

Almost all agreements provide specifically for modification or termination, and in many cases for both. Agreements are thus subject to the will and advantage of the contracting parties. Through such provisions the identity of the participating institutions is maintained and there are insured the powers conferred upon them by their charters and exercised through their separate corporate bodies. Only in cases where institutional charters provide for agreement is termination not possible without sanction by the state legislature.

Two agreements were found which provide that modification and termination may not take place. The first is the agreement between the Thomas W. Evans Museum and Dental Institute and the University of Pennsylvania. This agreement provides that the contract shall endure for a period of nine hundred and ninety-nine years. The second is the agreement between Barnard College and Columbia University. In the original contract provision was made that modification and termination could occur at the will of either party. Under amendment, however, effected in 1905, this provision was rescinded so far as it affected Barnard College.

In most cases, an agreement is to continue in force until modified or terminated, and no duration is specified for it. In certain agreements, however, the duration is specified. The agreement between the University of Chicago and the Otho S. A. Sprague Memorial Institute is to continue for fifty years unless altered, amended, or terminated. The duration of the agreement between the Perkins Observatory of Ohio Wesleyan University and the Yerkes Observatory of the University of Chicago is to be five years unless modified or terminated. The agreements between Harvard University and allied seminaries were voted by Harvard for a fixed period of time. Thus, the agreement with Boston University School of Theology was to endure for two years and the one with Newton Theological Institution for one year. These and the agreement with the Episcopal Theological School were later renewed for a period of three years. Since the elapse of this period they have continued in force, although no formal renewal of the agreements was found. The agreement with the Crane Theological School was also to endure for a period of two years. No renewal has apparently occurred, although the agreement is still in force. The agreement between Harvard University and the Massachusetts Institute of Technology continues in force, although it was made for but one year and has not been renewed. The effect of this practice by Harvard University is indefinite duration subject to modification or termination.

Agreements may be terminated by the mutual consent of the parties or by the withdrawal of one party subject to certain conditions as to notification. These conditions vary from agreement to agreement. They require in most cases notification in writing and this notification must be made at a stated period in advance of the time that the agreement is to be terminated. The usual period of notification is from five or six months to a year. An exception to this practice is the agreement between the Bouve School of Physical Education and Simmons College, which requires that the agreement be terminated only after four years' notice. The agreement between New York University and the National Academy of Design states that termination is not to affect the program of any student then enrolled from completing the combined course for the degree. The Harvard-Yale agreement states that notification prior to December first of any academic year shall terminate the agreement for all students not heretofore enrolled in the joint course.

Modification of inter-institutional agreements requires the action of the participating institutions. Thus the agreements entered into by Atlanta University with Morehouse and Spelman Colleges require for modification concurrent action of the respective boards. There is an interesting provision in the Atlanta University agreements in addition to the one which deals with modification. Before a new college may be admitted to the Atlanta System, sharing in the privileges accorded by the existing agreements, there must be joint approval by the boards of the respective institutions. Provision occurs in the agreement between the Otho S. A. Sprague Memorial Institute and the University of Chicago that alteration or amendment may be made by agreement between the contracting parties. The agreements between Columbia University and the College of Pharmacy, the New York Post-Graduate Medical School and Hospital, St. Stephen's College, and Teachers College may be modified at any time by mutual consent expressed in writing. The agreement between the Perkins Observatory of Ohio Wesleyan University and Ohio State University specifies that this agreement may be brought up for reconsideration by either contracting party and may be modified at the request of either party. The agreement between the Harvard Graduate School of Business Administration and the Yale Law School may be modified at any time by mutual consent.

SUMMARY

Provisions discussed in Chapter V relative to structure and function set up under agreement indicate that agreements may be formulated according to the needs and desires of participating institutions. Discussion of identity and powers indicates that agreements involve no loss of authority or autonomy on the part of participant institutions.

Agreements are consummated under the authority of the participating corporations and require no sanction by state legislatures. Institutional charters are neither modified nor surrendered nor is there any surrender of the powers granted by these charters.

Furthermore, agreements remain in force as long as they appear mutually advantageous. Should either institution feel that the existing agreement is no longer desirable, it may dissolve it or bring it up for modification. Modification occurs by mutual consent, but termination depends on the desire of only one party to the agreement.

Agreements involve no loss to institutional control of property or finances. Funds belonging to one institution remain under its full control, and restricted gifts or endowment are not endangered by the formation of agreements. In addition, one party to an agreement is under no obligation or responsibility for the debts, or future indebtedness, incurred by the other.

Finally, for the purpose of clarifying the relationship between institutions under agreement, special provisions may be included in the contract relative to control of students, preservation of institutional distinctive character, and maintenance of institutional standing. Agreements need involve no loss to institutional purposes or aims.

CHAPTER VII

Values Sought under Agreement

CHAPTERS IV, V, and VI of this study have discussed conditions fostering agreements, structure, and function set up under agreements and institutional identity and powers under agreement. Frequently in this discussion there has arisen the question of values. This problem will be treated in the present chapter.

Values, it must be borne in mind, are dependent on the various phases of the institutional situation. They differ from institution to institution and from agreement to agreement. Any classification of values is bound to do them violence inasmuch as they must be treated out of relationship to each other. The hope is held, however, that this list of values will indicate not only what values have been sought but what values may be sought where agreements are contemplated, are possible, or are even now in effect.

ENLARGED AND INCREASED OFFERINGS WITHOUT LOSS TO INSTITUTIONAL PROGRAMS

Through interchange, participating institutions are afforded enlarged and increased offerings. These do not detract from the quality or extensiveness of the institutional program, but instead provide opportunities and values for both the student and the institution.

Values for the Student

The student is afforded an opportunity to take work not offered in his own institution. This may be in the nature of elective courses pursued for the purpose of exploration and for the broadening of his general education. On the other hand, the courses taken in the allied institution may be courses of a specialized character which are required for a particular degree from his own institution or from the other. In such instances the courses may be pre-professional or professional in nature. They may be required in a combination course offered by both institutions. Thus, the student of an art or music school may enroll for theoretical work or for work in education in the allied institution qualifying him to teach. A student of a college or university may take courses in an allied school of education enabling him to meet the requirements for the high school certificate from the board of education of his particular state. Through agreement the student may supplement his professional training by work in a closely related professional field, such as a law course with business training, the work being directed toward this end by both institutions. The student may avail himself of opportunities for advanced courses not given at his own institution or for research provided by the facilities of the other institution. Interchange of courses has the additional advantage that it enables a student in a professional school, such as a theological school, who has not completed his undergraduate training, to obtain his undergraduate degree while studying for the advanced degree.

Values for the Institution

Wider provision for instruction in the smaller or more meagerly endowed institution enables it to provide a course of study more nearly approximating that of the best institution of the type in the country. Agreements thus strengthen the small college. The small college does not have to fear that students from its constituency will be attracted elsewhere because of its limited teaching personnel and equipment. In addition, several small colleges may benefit from agreements. Elementary and general courses can be combined, thus permitting specialists to concentrate on the advanced courses they are peculiarly fitted to teach and thereby extending the offerings of both institutions. Interchange of offerings also makes possible the teaching of certain courses on the frontiers of knowledge where, because of the small number in any one institution interested in them, their provision would not be otherwise possible. Important as this value is to the college, it is of especial importance to the university. Through agreement with another university or with an institute primarily for research, such an institution can extend the opportunities of its advanced students. Opportunities for interchange of offerings under agreement have advantage also for the founding of a new professional school or research institute. Where the endowment of such an institution is sufficient only to establish a school of medium standing, coordination with an established university may be employed to found an institution of high or even national reputation. Thus, through agreement, the new institution may be permitted to devote itself to specialized work in its field, the more general work and the work in the allied fields being offered by the university.

In addition, through interchange of offerings the services and influence of outstanding scholars may be made available to participating institutions. No longer is the work of the scholar of national or international reputation limited to the confines of but one institution. Students of allied institutions may enroll in his courses or he may give courses in the allied institution as part of his regular program. The participating institutions benefit from such practice in that the expense of his salary is shared and the cost of an instructional offering of such quality for each is decreased.

DECREASED INSTITUTIONAL EXPENSE WITH THE SAME OR INCREASED SERVICE

Agreements enable participating institutions to share certain expenses, liberating their funds for other purposes. Agreements also permit of decreased expense through differentiated programs or division of labor. Neither of these practices necessitates a decrease in quality or extent of service; in most cases they make possible increased service.

Economies may be effected in institutional programs, in administrative overhead, and in provision of facilities. Economies in program have been indicated in the discussion of institutional offerings. Economies in administrative overhead may result from the joint employment of administrative officers or through the serving of administrative officers in the allied institution without charge to that institution. Economies may result from unified services performed through one agency for the allied institutions. Thus, there may be a common bursary, publications and publicity service, registration and records service, health service, personnel service, placement service, and conduct of the summer session. There may be unified services such as heat, light, water, bookstore, purchasing, care of buildings and grounds. Furthermore, joint administration may lead to certain economies in the conduct of the affairs of an allied institution. Thus, the internal administration of a college may be modified by the wider experience and greater training that are afforded by a much larger administrative staff.

Administrative overhead may be decreased through the attraction of a larger number of students to the allied college. This may result from increased recognition and confidence achieved because of the agreement with the neighboring institution. It may result from direct cooperation of the neighboring institution in securing students, the recruiting and publicity service of the one being placed at the disposal of the other. It may result from the sending of students by the larger institution to the smaller. Frequently, a university has limited the size of its undergraduate body, turning away students who differ little in ability from those it accepts. In such cases, students are attracted to the allied institution by the assurance that its instruction is of the same quality as that of the university and by the fact that the graduates of the college receive the university degree or a degree endorsed by the university.

Administrative overhead may be decreased through the receipt of special gifts for carrying on part of the program of the allied institution, freeing other funds for other purposes. The securing of these gifts may result from increased confidence following the consummation of the agreement or through aid by the publicity and fund raising services of the university.

Administrative overhead for a university may be decreased through the avoidance of initial outlay and outlay for operation and maintenance in the case of a professional school of a particular type. Through incorporation of a given professional school in its educational system, the university is freed from expense in regard to the conduct of an institution of this type.

Decrease in expense may result from interchange of equipment or privileges with regard to buildings and other facilities. Thus an institution avoids the necessity of outlay for new equipment by sharing in the use of the equipment of the other institution. The complete expense for buildings and equipment may be avoided through joint outlay by the allied institutions. The sale of equipment under agreement by one institution to the other avoids the latter's outlay for new equipment. Operation and maintenance cost for buildings and equipment may be shared by both institutions or may be decreased for one institution through the assumption of its share by the other.

Under agreement an institution may obtain the use of apparatus and collections, libraries, laboratories for instruction and research, museums, classrooms, and classroom-buildings. In addition, auditoriums, athletic fields, gymnasiums, campus, chapel, administration buildings, and other buildings may be used jointly by allied institutions. Where institutions jointly use libraries, there may be avoided duplication in volumes and periodicals excepting those of constant and general usefulness. Dining halls and dormitories may be used in common.

PRESERVATION AND INCREASE IN STANDARDS OF ACHIEVEMENT

Retention of an institution's control over its program permits of no loss in quality as a result of agreements. Certain minimum standards are assumed through the contract. The allied institutions may raise their own standards as high as they find possible. In event of loss in standing by an allied institution, the other may bring the agreement up for modification, thereby limiting the relationship; or, if it thinks desirable, it may terminate the agreement at any time. Thus no danger to the quality of work carried on in one institution results from participation in agreements. Frequently, on the other hand, agreements lead to a rise in standards and to higher quality of work performed. This may be brought about in the following ways:

Faculty Interchange and Contact

Contact between members of the faculties of allied institutions broadens outlook and fosters exchange of ideas. Where a department of one institution consists of but one or two professors, contact with professors in the same department of the allied institution provides for many of the informal advantages of a larger staff. The faculty members of the isolated small college find such contacts of particular advantage. These contacts stimulate attack on common problems. They also develop a wholesome competitive feeling whereby members of allied institutions not only cooperate but also strive in their work to equal and surpass each other. It is this spirit of friendly rivalry which constitutes a major advantage in the formation of a group of undergraduate colleges associated together. Contacts between the staffs of allied institutions are often fostered by giving their members the same standing and affording them the same privileges with regard to faculty clubs and institutional facilities. In some cases, contact is fostered and the work of the institutions coordinated by offering scholarships in the allied university to junior members of the college staff working for higher degrees.

Contact is also of advantage to faculty members of different subject matter departments or different schools. A broader range of criticism is thereby established for the methods and achievements of allied institutions. Frequently, severe and continuous criticism arises and is brought to the attention of the institution in question. Where there is justification for such criticism, it is of value in redefining and clarifying standards; where the criticism is without foundation, it often leads to greater understanding of different fields of study.

Administration

The administrative standards in one institution prove an incentive to the administration of the other. Equal credit granted for equal work in a related institution implies that there shall be equal minimum standards. The tendency is to step standards up and make requirements uniform. The smaller institution gains much from association with the allied university. Standardization of minimum requirements occurs regarding admission, teaching load, salaries, selection of staff, credit allowed students, and requirements for degrees.

Joint Direction and Supervision on Administrative and Instructional Problems

Agreements provide specifically in many instances for joint direction and supervision of allied institutions. This may occur through interlocking directorates, election to boards of control, advisory committees, election of the same administrative officers, approval of staff appointments, representation on administrative and instructional councils, or the assumption of the direction and control of one institution for a specific period. Structure of this kind aids allied institutions to maintain minimum standards. Furthermore, similar action is brought about on common problems and the example and advice of one institution frequently stimulate the allied institution in dealing with its problems. Finally, a comprehensive program for the entire educational system or enterprise is made possible.

THE SAME OR INCREASED RECOGNITION FOR ALLIED INSTITUTIONS

The weaker institution gains in prestige from agreement with the stronger institution. The smaller institution gains in prestige from the larger institution. The larger and stronger institution frequently gains also because it is extending the opportunities it is affording its students and because it is taking into its program a specialized school or distinctive institution offering work of a type that it is not prepared to furnish.

Loss in prestige does not necessarily follow consummation of agreements with weaker institutions even where these are small four-year colleges. Agreements can be adapted to furthering the interests of these institutions, raising their standards, and developing an educational system for meeting more adequately the needs of the area and increasing the recognition afforded the larger and stronger institution. An example of just such practice was the formation of the Corporate Colleges of St. Louis University. The University has gained through the leadership it afforded the Corporate Colleges and through its help to them in achieving regional accreditation. Closer contact with these colleges has provided opportunities for their students to enter the University following graduation and for the continued employment on university tasks of their outstanding scholars or specialized facilities.

Furthermore, agreements need not lead to loss in prestige to the larger or stronger institution, because agreements frequently strengthen just those points in its offering which were inadequate. Agreements with professional schools of highly specialized types enable the university student to obtain instruction in a wider range of subjects than would be otherwise possible.

Finally, agreements bring into the university program institutions with distinctive character, which, although small and meager in resources, are attempting to provide unregimented training or training for different objectives from those that can be offered in the ordinary university program. Such institutions may fulfill a very important place in the general scheme of the university.

PRESERVATION AND AUGMENTATION OF INSTITUTIONAL DISTINCTIVE CHARACTER

Agreements enable institutions to preserve those characteristics which differentiate them from other institutions. Not only are characteristics preserved under agreement but in many cases they are augmented and the institutions are enabled to realize their distinctive objectives to a greater degree than otherwise would be the case. Discussion of distinctive character emphasizes three types of value:

General Values for the Student

Under agreement, the separate college is enabled to preserve the institutional life and activities of its student body. A feeling of unity is maintained which is less possible where all form their loyalties primarily to the university. Above all, the characteristics of the small college are preserved. The small college is spoken of by some as the most effective educational unit.[1] Yale and Harvard are attempting to break up their large student bodies into colleges under the house-plan. According to this plan each college remains an integral part of the university. Under agreement long-established colleges continue to direct their own programs and develop their distinctive contributions.

Preservation of the small college enables its students of like training and purpose to continue to live in close intimacy on their separate campus and in their own residence halls. They continue to enjoy out-of-class contacts with instructors and with administrative staff of the institution. There is not the danger that the undergraduate student will be set adrift in the large student body of a great university. The preservation of the small college insures the individual and personal acquaintance of members of the staff with each student. Through such contact the student's efforts and achievement can be better estimated. Regulations can be adapted to individual circumstance, and opportunity is presented for stimulation of scholarship through personal contact and for sound educational and vocational guidance. Furthermore, the organized life of the student body is preserved. The small college continues the supervision of undergraduate activities. Participation in and direction of extra-curricular activities to a much greater degree is assured the individual student than if he were a member of a larger body. The undergraduate woman's college retains its separate campus and activities. Women students carry on their own institutional life and direct their own activities distinct from the allied institution and yet are members of it. Students of the theological school retain their own activities and their own institutional life. Under agreement, graduate instruction is concentrated in one place, affording graduate students separate institutional life apart from contact with undergraduates and undergraduate activities.

[1] Blaisdell, James A, "Claremont Colleges; Some Educational Purposes and Results." *The Association of American Colleges Bulletin,* Vol. XVI, No. 1, March 1930.

General Values for Instruction

Each institution under agreement continues to direct the instruction which it offers. It preserves in this manner the characteristics which differentiate its program as a separate institution. The denominational college continues to give the moral and religious instruction desired by its constituency and for which it was founded. The undergraduate college or the professional school employs under agreement its own methods and techniques. As an independent institution allied with another it preserves the right to institute such methods as honors courses and to follow out other devices which have educational promise for its students. In addition, the individual college, linked through agreement, is free to undertake an experimental program whereby it can specialize in certain fields or adapt its instruction to a particular type of student. Its ability to specialize is fostered by the fact that it continues to be under its own board of control thoroughly in sympathy with its distinctive purposes. Through agreement, however, specialists from the faculty of the larger institution are available for its use and development and there is always possible the advice and counsel of the larger institution in the improvement of program and the definition of objectives.

Coordination through agreement does not lead to bureaucracy and standardization, which are possible in a large university under a single board of control and a unified administration. The professional school continues in close contact with the members of its particular profession, enjoying their supervision and advice in the regulation and development of its program. The denominational college maintains its contacts with the theological seminary, the churches, and its sectarian constituency.

Values of a More Intangible Nature

The distinctive background of the allied college is maintained. Each institution develops those intangible characteristics which play a large part in the educative offering. In addition, each institution preserves its traditions, customs, campus, and location. Where the location is rural, affording beautiful surroundings, there is the assurance under agreement that this advantage will be retained. Furthermore, through the preservation of distinctive character, the good will and support of alumni and constituency are preserved. The maintenance of institutional character fosters the retention of loyalties.

PRESERVATION OF IDENTITY AND POWERS UNDER AGREEMENT

The values enumerated under this heading represent a recapitulation of the discussion in Chapter VI. Under agreements, institutions retain their separate legal identity. No change occurs in charters, nor do participating institutions relinquish the powers accorded by these. Furthermore, allied institutions retain full control over property and finances. They assume no liability for the debts of each other. There is no danger to endowments or trust funds of either institution from the consummation of agreements. Each institution supports its corporate organization and its faculty. In addition, agreements are subject to modification and termination by the contracting parties. Should the contract appear to work to the disadvantage of either one, that institution may terminate the agreement or amend it following a prescribed course of action. Institutions may thus consummate agreements during a period of trial and experimentation, to be followed later by closer coordination or resumption of separate institutional status. Finally, institutions may limit the degree of coordination effected and insure identity and powers by regulations as to the degree to which control, administration, faculty, and facilities are to be coordinated.

COOPERATIVE PLANNING OF HIGHER EDUCATION FOR AN AREA

Not only are values for the institution sought under agreement but also values for the area. The founding and development of independent institutions have frequently led to overlapping of programs and competitive effort to win students and support. Institutional loyalties have outweighed loyalty to the constituency as a whole. In consequence, there has been little cooperative planning of higher education under independent development. Agreements afford opportunities for intensive and prolonged investigation of the needs of the area. They lead to the determination of the place of each institution in the area's program. Through agreements differentiation is possible. There is also possible the development of new service. Through inter-institutional agreements the citizens of the area become united behind a single educational program, insuring them adequate provision of higher educational opportunities and the wise and economical use of contributions made to the development of higher education. The inter-institutional agreement is a highly effective instrument for cooperative planning.

POSSIBLE LOSS OF VALUES

Some arguments are raised against larger groupings and larger institutions. Below is presented a statement which sets forth very concisely one such criticism:

The executive and administrative point of view thus tends to obscure the scholarly point of view—a change that has taken place almost everywhere in American universities. . . . But, even so, universities do not stop growing. Unaware apparently of the pit into which they are stumbling, they grow bigger still, adding or annexing schools, institutes and even affiliated institutions, most of them useless, or unsuitable, and all of them expensive if, however unfit, they are properly carried on. At this stage excessive concentration gives way to disintegration; for no one knows or can possibly know what is happening in our overgrown universities.[2]

Starting from the same observed premise, as has this study, that there is a strong tendency among higher educational institutions toward coordination and integration, the questions raised above are those of values. Is this tendency dangerous? Is it dangerous to the university, to higher education, and to society as a whole? The questions which are pertinent to this study are those dealing with the joining of higher educational institutions by agreement. The founding of new schools under an existing board does not come within the scope of this study.

Do agreements lead to "disintegration," that is, to a condition where the component parts of the educational system are not correlated, are not of the same standing and are not engaged in furthering the common task? Conceivably, where large numbers of schools are placed under a single board and a single administration, they may lack adequate direction and management, since the available supervision is extended to care for the needs of each. Under agreements, however, as was seen in Chapter V, each institution retains its own board of control and its own administration. Each institution is, therefore, under the direction and management of those who have its welfare especially at heart. The university built through agreements is not a vast combination of resources escaping the well-intentioned efforts of a single person or a small group of persons to direct the purposes for which each institution was founded. Instead, it is a system of schools, cooperating and yet independent, which does not depend upon the close supervision of any one officer for its effective functioning.

[2] Flexner, Abraham, "The University in American Life." *The Atlantic Monthly*, Vol. 152; No. 5, p. 622, May 1932.

This concept of a university, as was pointed out (on page 49) in the citation from Bosworth and Jones, permits its various schools greater opportunity to realize their distinctive aims. Under such structure, the tendency for the executive and administrative point of view to obscure the scholarly point of view need not obtain. There is less tendency toward the bureaucracy and standardization that prevail where a single board attempts to control all the several units in a large organization. These semi-independent units co-operate for their mutual welfare. Not all of them, however, form connections of the same intimacy. For some the relationship is very loose, certain resources being placed at the service of the university and the remainder of their facilities being held for their own distinctive needs. In the case of others, the relationship is extremely close through the agency of coordinated control and administration. But all of these relationships are subject to mutual advantage. Should it appear to either participant in an agreement that the relationship works a disadvantage, that institution may withdraw or bring up the contract for modification. Cooperation under an agreement is therefore a means of mobilizing the facilities of all to their individual and common advantage, and to the advantage of society.

Nor are such "affiliated" schools, institutes, and institutions necessarily expensive to the university. As was pointed out in Chapter VI, each, under agreement, may be financially independent. The university assumes no responsibility for the debts of its allied schools nor is it necessarily under any financial obligation for their maintenance. Rather, the burden for the university in its effort to provide adequately for the area may be lightened. Through agreement, funds which otherwise must be employed to provide certain instruction or to operate certain schools may be released and made available for the more effective operation of its remaining program or for the establishment of new enterprise.

What educational offering and what educational organization do not belong in the university scheme? Such a question is beyond the scope of this study. To contend that all schools that have formed agreements have a place in the university would take the discussion far afield and would prove in all probability unproductive. This much, however, can be said: Not all the types of schools listed in Table IV are "useless" or "unsuitable" for the university. Whatever changes occur in the university in future, agreements may be of service in linking the desirable offerings of independent schools to the university.

Meanwhile, since the university is seeking to offer the diverse types of training which it does at present, the agreement is a particularly useful instrument. It is economical for society. Many of the schools which are carrying on specialized endeavor need university offerings to supplement their programs. Unless institutions have recourse to university facilities, these offerings must be provided at great expense elsewhere, thus resulting in the support by society of duplicated enterprise.

The question whether unsuitable or useless courses carried on by the university injure the quality of work carried on by its other departments also lies beyond the scope of his study. If this contention has basis and as it is more clearly demonstrated, then the university can take steps toward freeing itself from such activities. Under agreement the university has greater opportunity to effect these changes than under unified control. Not only can it terminate the agreement, but it can modify it, setting up greater and greater restrictions both as to quality of students it admits and as to the courses for which they are eligible.

CHAPTER VIII

Some Characteristics of Undesirable Agreements

THE documents on which this study is based throw little light on characteristics which may be regarded as making for undesirable agreements. Where an agreement has been modified at a later date or where it has been abrogated, however, there are indications in many cases of types of agreement which are open to question. Where agreements have repeatedly stressed certain safeguards for institutional identity and powers, there is by implication an index to what constitutes an undesirable agreement. Finally certain material has been of assistance in supplementing the conclusions drawn from direct reference to the agreements themselves. Of particular importance for this purpose is the Annual Report for 1928 of the Cleveland Conference for Educational Cooperation—the chapter dealing with general principles.[1]

FROM THE STANDPOINT OF SOCIETY

1. Agreements would seem to be undesirable if they serve to perpetuate institutions incapable of offering work of satisfactory quality. An institution whose offerings are inferior may extend through cooperation with other institutions the opportunities afforded its students, and in this manner it may be able to survive for a longer or shorter period. If, however, such an institution continues under cooperation to provide training of low standard, the desirability of the agreement is at least open to question.

Certain of the agreements which have been studied had for one immediate purpose the raising of standards in the weaker institutions. Thus, St. Louis University aided its Corporate Colleges to reorganize their programs and win accreditation. Three of these, Fontbonne, Maryville, and Webster, after a two-year probationary period following the consummation of the agreements, were placed

[1] *The Cleveland Conference for Educational Cooperation, Annual Reports and Reports of Committees, 1928.* The Cleveland Conference for Educational Cooperation, Cleveland, Ohio, 1928.

on the approved list by the North Central Association of Colleges and Secondary Schools. Another, Chaminade College, apparently could not make the necessary adjustment. It was subsequently closed and the agreement terminated. The evidence would seem to indicate that cooperation between this weak institution and the University, except as a means of helping it to raise its standards, was looked upon with disfavor.[2]

2. Agreements may be undesirable when they perpetuate certain institutional offerings of inferior quality, even though the remainder of the program of the participating institutions is satisfactory.

3. Agreements would seem to be undesirable also if they are employed to inaugurate new enterprise of low standard. Frequently degree courses and even new institutions have been established by means of the agreement. From the standpoint of society such cooperation would seem to be questionable where the new enterprise is of low quality.

4. Agreements would seem to be undesirable where they perpetuate unnecessary duplication of institutional offerings. This viewpoint is borne out by explicit and implicit provisions in the agreements studied. The agreement between Colorado College and Broadmoor Art Academy has for an avowed aim the elimination of duplication and competition between the two institutions. Certain of the agreements provide for differentiation of institutional programs. Certain others limit the courses in another institution in which a student may enroll to those not provided in his own institution. The agreement which throws open all courses in one institution to students enrolled in another would appear to be, therefore, undesirable in most cases.

FROM THE STANDPOINT OF HIGHER EDUCATIONAL INSTITUTIONS

1. Agreements may be undesirable from the institutional standpoint when the benefits from them accrue to but one party to the agreement. Certain institutions reported that the agreements in which they participated were considered by them of little value, and one university stated that the abrogation of these agreements was even now under consideration.

2. Agreements appear to be undesirable when they involve for one institution expense that is not compensated for by the benefits

[2] *Bulletin of St. Louis University,* Catalog Number, Vol. XVII, No. 2, February 1931.

received. The specific provisions appearing in many agreements with regard to remuneration for services rendered imply that agreements as far as possible should rest on a *quid pro quo* basis. Periodically it seems advisable that each institution should report to the other all expenses incurred by virtue of the agreement in order that an adjustment can be effected.

3. Agreements would seem to be undesirable if through them the contracting parties are compelled to assume obligations which were not set forth in the terms of cooperation. Freedom from certain obligations is specified in many agreements. Thus, an institution is not to be considered liable for the support, management, or debts of another. One institution is not to be required to offer courses for the benefit of the students of the other if its own students do not demand them. An institution is not to be compelled to admit unqualified students to its courses by virtue of the agreement, and any student who has been excluded from one institution shall not gain admission to its courses by being enrolled in the other. An institution is to have final voice regarding the teaching load of its faculty members and the use to be made of its equipment, and other facilities.

4. Agreements would seem to be undesirable when they involve conflict of authority between institutions respecting control of finances, programs, or students. Study of the agreements appears to support the belief that agreements should define as clearly as possible which institution is to have deciding voice in any situation which leads to division of control and possible conflicts of interest.

5. Agreements are undesirable when they involve loss of good will for either of the contracting parties. Agreements which involve loss of or diminution of loyalties of alumni and constituencies are open to question. Agreements which lend themselves to exploitation of the reputation of one institution for the benefit of the other are undesirable.

6. Agreements may be undesirable when they are formed between institutions whose aims and objectives are fundamentally antagonistic. One of the agreements in this study, between a theological school and a university, was reported as raising doubts in the minds of friends of both institutions. It was claimed that the aim of the theological school was to evangelize its students and that this prevented the cooperation set forth in its agreement with the university.

CHAPTER IX

Cooperative Planning in Higher Education

ALTHOUGH the texts of agreements bear little direct reference to cooperative planning, it was felt that the agreement as a means of coordinating the work of higher educational institutions held certain implications that should as far as possible be indicated. The decision was made, in consequence, to include in this study a brief discussion of cooperative planning in higher education.

Cooperative planning in higher education will, in all probability, make use of various methods for the development of a unified program. Not only will it employ the inter-institutional agreement, but also the merger, differentiation of institutional offerings, restriction of offerings, elimination of duplication between institutional programs, relocation of certain institutions, and even the abandonment of some which seem to be unable to make a worthwhile contribution. These so-called methods are not to be regarded as mutually exclusive. In many situations they may be used in combination, and in almost all cases cooperative planning will make use of several of them. They have been enumerated here for the purpose of distinguishing between them and also because of the light which they throw on the characteristics of the inter-institutional agreement.

The source material for this discussion is the pertinent educational literature and also the documents describing the terms of agreements. The point may be raised whether evidence based on the structure of agreements, as set forth in the documents, is sufficient to indicate their function in planning higher education. Obviously a study of structure has limitations which can only be offset by an examination, which would lie beyond the scope of the present study, of agreements as they operate in practice. On the other hand, a study of structure presents certain empirical evidence that is worthy of consideration. Where structure has remained unmodified over a period of time in the face of the possibility for modification, there would seem to be indication that this structure has been found of value and that it is probably of value in coordination and cooperative planning. The present discussion purports to be simply an approach to the problem of planning in higher education. It is hoped that in future other studies will be made both of the agreement as it functions in operation and of its implications for a planned program.

A planned program for higher education, whether established for the individual institution or for a group of institutions, would seem to have the following major objectives: 1) provision of worthwhile and justifiable offerings to meet the needs of the expected constituency; 2) provision of adequate range of offerings to meet these needs; 3) provision of high quality service in all lines or fields that are presented; 4) economical use of resources that are available. In addition, such a program should attempt to insure: 1) availability of all facilities for the training for which they can most effectively be used; 2) elimination of unnecessary duplication of offerings and facilities; 3) elimination of unnecessary overhead in the provision of offerings; 4) development of means for insuring the continued effectiveness of higher educational services.

On the basis of these objectives, it would seem that an institution might attempt independently to improve its services by the following means:

1. Augmentation of resources, thereby improving and adding to its facilities and offerings.

2. Reduction in overhead through various methods of reorganizing the instructional program, such as development of divisional organization in place of departmental organization; development of comprehensive courses; establishment of larger classes; elimination of duplication in content of courses; etc.[1]

3. Elimination of courses which do not form a central part of its program. Such offerings might be certain elective courses, highly specialized courses, or courses which are relatively expensive because of the small number of students enrolling in them.

4. Elimination of offerings which are provided as effectively or more effectively by other institutions serving the same area or constituency.[2]

[1] Hill, David S. and Kelly, Fred J., *Economy in Higher Education*, pp. 56-71. The Carnegie Foundation for the Advancement of Teaching, New York, 1933.

[2] "Too often when higher institutions look at their neighbors to find out what these neighbors are doing, the purpose is not to avoid the duplication of functions but to rival or surpass through imitation. This is the besetting professional sin of

5. Restriction of its entire program to a field which can be provided with a high degree of effectiveness. In this manner the four-year college can be reorganized as a junior college, or a university might eliminate certain of its schools which it was not in position to support effectively.

6. Differentiation of its program through emphasis upon a particular portion that it is peculiarly fitted to offer.

7. Removal to a new location where it will not be faced with keen competition for students and support.

8. Development of new objectives better adapted to the needs of its expected and desired constituency.

On the basis of the same objectives, it would seem that an institution in cooperation with other institutions might improve its services through:

1. Cooperative action for securing support and gifts.

2. Cooperative control and management of resources and program as under coordinated control and administration.

3. Extension of offerings afforded its students through opportunities made available in other institutions.

4. Development of combination courses with other institutions providing training not formerly offered by either institution.

5. Enlargement of its instructional staff through part-time employment of teachers in other institutions.

6. Establishment of joint administrative offices and services.

7. Extension of opportunities along non-instructional lines through offerings made available in other institutions.

8. Extension of opportunities afforded staff members through the facilities of other institutions.

9. Elimination of certain offerings which duplicate the offerings in other institutions. Instances of this are reported among institutions in the Philadelphia and Pittsburgh areas.[3]

---

our higher academic planning. Those responsible for our higher education need to turn their backs once and for all upon that institutional provincialism which encourages every academic ambition which might appeal to president, faculty or trustees. To feel that nothing outside one's own institution is important leads inevitably to dissipation of the social wealth of the community available for the support of higher education, whether collected through taxes or through gifts."— Henry Suzzallo, in *Twenty-eighth Annual Report of the President and of the Treasurer*, pp. 3-4. The Carnegie Foundation for the Advancement of Teaching, New York, 1933.

[3] Kelly, Robert L., "The College and National Recovery." *The Bulletin of the Association of American Colleges*, Vol. XIX, No. 3, p. 291, November 1933.

10. Restriction in the scope of program, an institution limiting itself to work that it can carry on with a high degree of effectiveness. Under agreement, an institution may restrict itself to the first two years of the college course, to the upper two years, or to graduate instruction. A similar practice may occur under consolidation where two campuses are maintained by the single board of control.[4]

11. Consolidation of one of its schools with a similar independent school, the merged institution linked to it by agreement.

12. Consolidation of a certain department in one institution with a similar department in another institution, resulting in the linking of the new institution to each of the former institutions through agreement.

13. Consolidation with another institution, forming a new institution of higher standard and greater effectiveness. A university may consolidate an independent school with one of its own, thus making its own school more effective.

14. Differentiation of program made possible through availability of offerings in other institutions.

15. Development of a new or distinctive program made possible by cooperation with other institutions.

16. Relocation in close proximity to another institution, making possible interchange of offerings and other cooperative practice.

On the basis of the objectives noted above, it would seem that several institutions acting in cooperation might plan higher educational provision for the same area and constituency through:

1. Combined study of the resources, programs, and objectives of institutions serving the area and constituency.

2. Combined study of the present and future needs of the area and constituency.

3. Formulation of a plan to promote the development of effective higher educational provision for the area and constituency.

4. Establishment of some form of cooperative structure or organization to promote the continued working out of the accepted program.

It would seem that such an organization might attempt to accomplish the aims of the general program through recommendations regarding the following:

1. Types of service that institutions either individually or collec-

---

[4] Reynolds, J. H., "The Trinity System." A leaflet published by Hendrix-Henderson College in 1933.

tively might undertake to meet the needs of the area and constituency.

2. The contributions that each of the institutions might make to the general program.

3. Means by which each institution might make its own contribution more effective.

4. Effective means by which the various institutions might coordinate their efforts.

5. The geographical needs of the area for higher educational provision.

6. Abandonment of certain institutions which appear to be unable to contribute to the general program because of inferior and low grade offerings or offerings which apparently are not justified in the light of the needs of the area and constituency.

In formulating a list of ways in which there can be worked out cooperative planning of higher educational provision, the assumption has been made that planning is most likely to develop within the so-called area or region. Cooperative planning may develop, of course, through a program for higher education worked out for the nation as a whole. It would seem to be more probable, however, for the area or region because of the individualistic and local character of higher institutions. In addition, such development would receive impetus from movements toward regional and city planning to be observed in various portions of the country. Thus, there seems the strong possibility that such areas as a metropolitan region, a state, or a group of neighboring communities will prove the laboratories for the working out of cooperative planning in higher education.

In such areas, planning will probably develop gradually through combined efforts to provide worth-while and adequate offerings. A single institution, such as a university which has achieved high standing and large concentration of resources, may take the lead in such development, or two such institutions may inaugurate a plan of cooperation which in time is broadened to include the other institutions of the area.

In any such development of a planned program account will have to be taken of the fact that there are probably certain institutions unable to provide offerings of even minimum standard. Such institutions may be four-year colleges of very limited enrollment; they may be institutions of greatly depleted resources, or institutions heavily in debt; they may be secondary schools which have aspired to the rôle of colleges but lack proper facilities. Inferior institutions almost universally will be found unable to contribute effectively to the planned program for the area. Not only will they be unable to make a contribution but they will render in reality a disservice by preventing students from obtaining the kind of training that is required. Institutions of low standard, it seems probable therefore, should in the interests of society be closed. Abandonment of such institutions will tend to increase the quality of all higher educational provision, and will also free the resources of the area from the necessity of supporting inferior programs.

Another case for abandonment may be the institution whose program no longer meets a need sufficient to justify its continuance. A denominational college may have lost its constituency owing to the fact that the constituency moved away or its members are no longer attracted by the denominational character of the institution but study at other institutions. Where such a college fails to make a contribution and yet may not be reorganized readily to play an effective part in the area's program, it should probably be closed.

Abandonment may be desirable in the case of certain institutions whose offerings duplicate the programs of other institutions, thus providing excess of training along the same lines. There are frequently too many colleges within the area to serve the needs of the population or there are several professional schools of the same type, each competing with the others and struggling for existence. It would seem that in the interest of the general program certain of these institutions should be closed.

Individualistic development of higher education has undoubtedly fostered inferior institutions, institutions of limited appeal, and institutions which duplicate unnecessarily services rendered the same constituency. Abandonment should, of course, follow upon thorough investigation of the institutions in question and of the needs of the area. In certain cases institutions may be reorganized in such a way that they continue to play an effective part in the area's program. But abandonment should not be looked upon simply as the last resort in the case of institutions whose programs are inferior or unjustified. Abandonment should be considered a necessary means in certain instances of insuring the development of an effective program for the area.

Reorganization of higher institutions and adaptation to the needs of the area may be accomplished in many ways. One of the most effective means will be restriction of institutional programs. Restriction of offerings is of service where an institution spreads its efforts over too wide a field for the resources at its disposal. Thus, the four-year college might be reorganized as a junior college. Harper, in speaking of this possibility, said, "It is surely a higher thing to do honest and thorough work in a lower field than to fall short of such work in a higher field."[5] Restriction of offerings, on the other hand, may lead a college to limit itself to the upper years of its course or to graduate instruction. Restriction may also lead an institution simply to eliminate certain offerings which do not form a central portion of its program.

Restriction of offerings may be carried on independently by an institution as a means of increasing the effectiveness of its program. On the other hand, it may be carried on in cooperation with the other institutions of the area. Thus, restriction of offerings may be employed to eliminate duplication of institutional services. As such, it represents a primary step in coordinating the work in higher education of the area. Avoidance of duplication through restriction of offerings lays the foundation for the development of the general program and makes possible the development of cooperation between the various institutions. Restriction of offerings frequently occurs, therefore, in the employment of the inter-institutional agreement.

Another means for the reorganization of higher institutions and for adapting them to the needs of the area is differentiation of institutional offerings. Through differentiation a college emphasizes that portion of the general program that it is most able to offer. One college may devote itself primarily to work in the natural sciences; another to the social sciences; another to literature and fine arts, or languages. Two advantages for the institution are sought through differentiation: first, the college is able to establish outstanding facilities in the line of its chief endeavor; second, it takes itself out of competition with other institutions, thus making possible the development of a distinctive contribution to the area's program. As Cottrell remarks,

There is in this question of differentiation the one appropriate point for us to observe the potentialities of cooperative planning on a national basis for

[5] Harper, William R., *The Trend in Higher Education*, p. 378. University of Chicago Press, Chicago, 1905.

collegiate education. Some institutions which are now dying because they cannot bear the full load of offering work of distinction on many lines might well be assigned a certain emphasis in which they could excel and in this contribution they would continue an important function in the provision of collegiate education for the nation.[6]

Differentiation, as conceived by Cottrell, is differentiation of emphasis and not differentiation of offerings except as the latter may be accomplished to a degree through concentration on one field. The differentiated institution continues to give instruction in all fields that make up the liberal arts course. Emphasis in the one field does not absolve it from obligation to present minimum elementary and advanced offerings in other fields. Thus, in the case of the inferior institution whose offerings are of low quality, differentiation holds out little hope of achieving adequate adjustment. Before an inferior institution may develop distinctive opportunities in a narrower field of endeavor it will have to raise almost all its offerings to satisfactory standard.

Differentiation holds out greater opportunities for the college whose standards are acceptable or even superior. Even there the question arises, however, whether the single institution can differentiate its program unless it has large resources to devote to the purpose. It is still compelled to offer elementary and general courses in practically all fields. It will probably have to provide also enough facilities in the unemphasized fields to meet the advanced needs of its student body. In spite of even a rigorous admissions program, there is always the possibility that the interests of certain students will lead them to wish to supplement their work by advanced offerings in other fields. To differentiate its program successfully, the single institution should make sufficient provision in all offerings to meet its students' needs. Thus there is the question whether even the superior institution can alone differentiate its program without recourse to additional funds.

Emphasis upon one field, where it involves withdrawal of opportunity from other fields, rests upon the availability of full facilities in those other fields in case of need. Differentiation carried on independently would seem to be fraught with difficulties. Where institutions are members of a group, however, the possibilities for developing superior and distinctive offerings are very large. As a

[6] Cottrell, Donald P., "Present Problems in College Administration." *The New York Times*, August 10, 1931.

member of a group, an institution may cut down its offerings in the unemphasized fields or eliminate them entirely, proceeding on the assurance that they will be available in the programs of co-operating institutions. Three or four colleges which, under agreement, would each choose a different field of emphasis could thereby build a united program of outstanding opportunity for the area. But the single institution would be unable to differentiate its program unless it had extensive resources which might be devoted to the purpose. Thus, where the single institution was inferior in standing, differentiation would seem to be impracticable; where the inferior institution was one of a group, all of which were attempting to differentiate their programs, the field assigned to the inferior institution would be the weak portion of the general program. To sum up, then, differentiation seems to offer little advantage for the institution acting alone, unless it can draw from additional sources of income; as a member of a group an inferior institution may profit from differentiation but even there its offerings are likely to be inferior to the offerings of the rest; to be most effective, differentiation should be carried on cooperatively by several institutions each of which is already of recognized standing.

As was pointed out in the introductory chapter, the ability to specialize institutional offerings depends in large measure upon the ability to supplement them where necessary from the other offerings of the particular institution or from the offerings of other institutions and agencies. Recognition seems to be growing among higher educational institutions that they are not able to provide independently all the facilities demanded of them. Even the college which offers outstanding opportunities is realizing apparently that the needs of its students require facilities which it is not in position to offer and, in consequence, it is sending its students elsewhere for the additional training they need. The following announcement, for example, is made in the Bulletin of Bennington College:

> During the last two years those students who, in order to explore their special fields, need facilities which the College cannot itself offer, will be encouraged to go to centers where there are the best opportunities for continuing major work under the general supervision of the College. This plan will apply to those who need laboratory research facilities offered by certain universities; to those who wish to study national and international affairs in such centers as Washington, London and Geneva; and to those who desire

to study foreign languages and literatures abroad or to gain access to the leading centers of art or music.[7]

It would seem that the cooperative planning of higher education for the area would not make necessary, except in a comparatively few cases, sending students to national or international centers for the training needed. In most cases students can be sent to neighboring institutions. The institutions of the area can restrict certain of their offerings in those fields in which they are least competent and send their students to other institutions where such provision is of high quality. Such restriction of offerings may or may not result in differentiation. It may simply decrease the burden carried by the college.

Another means of bringing about coordination in the interest of a general program is the consolidation or merger. The consolidation has frequently been looked upon as a means of increasing institutional facilities. At the same time and possibly to a greater extent it should be regarded as a means of eliminating competition.

Institutions may well be merged where they offer identical programs. Consolidation makes possible economy for the area inasmuch as it tends to do away with duplication of administrative overhead. Under consolidation institutional plants may be closed and equipment and services combined. This would seem to be advisable where possible since society should not be called upon to support unnecessary duplication of enterprise. Thus, two professional schools of the same type should be merged; two liberal arts colleges may well be consolidated where practically all their offerings are identical; even two colleges of different denominations, the greater part of whose offerings have no denominational flavor, may be consolidated, as in the case of Intermountain Union College.[8]

Consolidation may well prove desirable where institutions are supported by the same constituency, as two colleges drawing support from the same denominational board. Two colleges located in the same city and making appeals to the same chamber of commerce and to the same industries may find it desirable to merge. Consolidation would seem to be desirable among public institutions within the same state and drawing their support from the same legislature.

[7] *Bennington College Bulletin:* Announcement for the Second Year, 1933-1934, Vol. 1, No. 4, p. 24, May 1933.

[8] As reported in the annual catalog of Intermountain Union College.

Consolidation may be desirable where the endowment of two institutions is for the most part unrestricted and where there are no limiting stipulations which prevent merging.

Consolidation may possibly be desirable where difference in standards prevents the formation of agreements. Thus, instead of linking two institutions of different standards through cooperation, it may be better to merge them and establish a single program of high quality. On the other hand, where one of the institutions is of inferior or distinctly poor standard, that institution should probably be closed. The merging of such an institution with an established high grade institution is of doubtful value to the superior institution or to higher educational provision for the area. Often in the case of the inferior institution any assets are already eaten up by indebtedness and liabilities. To merge such an institution with an institution which is already offering an acceptable program would only seem to increase the burden of the latter without substantially adding to its resources. The superior institution is compelled to administer the property of the other, to care for the other's students, to maintain the other's records, and to adopt its alumni. The history of many institutions shows one or more mergers, but aside from eliminating competition, which might have been accomplished through abandonment, there probably followed in many of these cases slight advantage. The same principle seems to hold true for two institutions of inferior standing. Merging them will not in many cases give rise to a single institution of high standing. In the interest of society and of the constituency of these institutions, it would seem better to close them and send their students elsewhere to obtain the desired training.

Consolidation may be desirable where the distinctive characteristics of the institutions in question are not sufficient to justify their continuance under separate control and administration.

Consolidation may be desirable where coordination of programs has been found advisable and where there seems little likelihood that the demand will arise for the resumption of separate institutional status. Seldom following a merger is it possible to reestablish the independence of the participating institutions.[9]

Another means which may be employed in increasing the effectiveness of higher educational provision is relocation. Relocation

[9] A case where institutions have merged and then resumed independent status is that of Transylvania College and the College of the Bible.

frequently takes an institution out of competition with other institutions. It enables the establishment of higher educational provision in a portion of the area which at present lacks facilities for higher learning. The enlarged demand for the opportunities afforded by the institution, in consequence, makes possible more effective use of its resources. As a result of relocation, an institution frequently gains in strength and more adequate higher educational provision is thereby afforded the area. For example,

One of the most recent cases of this type [relocation] in the group of colleges being studied is that of the College of the Pacific which moved to a new location at Stockton, California, only six or seven years ago. Today no one connected with the institution doubts that the move was wise, and it is clearly evident that the college has entered upon a larger field of service than was possible for it before.[10]

On the other hand, relocation may be employed to bring institutions in close proximity to each other, thereby making possible interchange of facilities. In such cases relocation is employed as a preliminary step toward the development of the inter-institutional agreement.

The methods which have been considered thus far—abandonment, restriction of offerings, differentiation, consolidation, and relocation—make possible the development of higher standard offerings for the area while at the same time they serve to eliminate duplication and competition between independent institutions. They do not, however, join the institutions of the area together in a unified program. The only one of these methods which might lead to such a unified program is the merger, and the employment of the merger for this purpose is probably impossible in most cases because of differences in tradition and control which serve to divide higher educational institutions.

The employment of the merger alone for the development of a unified program would necessitate the establishment of a single mammoth institution to supply all the higher educational needs of the area. Instead of such practice it seems probable that a certain number of institutions will endure, each functioning under its own board of trustees. The number of such institutions may be smaller than at present because of the abandonment of certain institutions and the consolidation of others. This conclusion, however, does

[10] Reeves, F. W. and Others, *The Liberal Arts College, Based on Surveys of Thirty-five Colleges Related to the Methodist Episcopal Church*, p. 37. University of Chicago Press, 1932.

not appear certain. The number may be as large or perhaps larger because there is strong probability that new institutions will be founded from time to time to care for needs that are not otherwise satisfied. In either case it would seem that the area must continue to support a certain number of independently controlled higher educational institutions and that cooperation between these, which is required for the functioning of a unified program, must be effected through the agreement. Agreements would seem to be advisable in the following situations:

1. Agreements between institutions of high academic standing are advisable. Institutional welfare and the welfare of the area seem to indicate that only offerings of adequate standing are supplemented by the provisions of other institutions. Supplementation of weak offerings probably renders a disservice to society and to the institutions themselves, preventing necessary changes in quality of offerings and fostering the dependence of one institution on the other.

2. Agreements should be formed between institutions whose offerings tend to be dissimilar. Coordination of institutions whose programs are identical would probably better take place through the merger, since the merger serves to eliminate duplication of administrative and instructional overhead. Thus, the agreement may be of value between the college and the professional school, between the college and the university, between two professional schools of different types, between a college for men and a college for women, and between two colleges of broadly differing emphases.

3. Agreements would seem to be desirable where retention of the individual character of separate institutions is demanded. The continuance of the small college, the denominational college, the experimental college, the college free from the evils of bureaucracy, the institution with a tradition of long service and good will may be achieved through the agreement.

4. Agreements would seem to be advisable where restricted endowment and special gifts prevent merging and consolidation.

5. Agreements may be formed between institutions where coordination is looked upon as still in an experimental stage. Agreements make possible easy readjustment and termination of the relationship should need arise.

6. Finally, agreements are of service in the establishment of new institutions through cooperation afforded thereby in control and

administration as well as in offerings. An established institution may be of very great aid in the development of a new and distinctive type of institution designed to meet special needs not already provided for in the area.

As has been pointed out the agreement is the method which seems to hold out greatest opportunities for coordinating the many different types of higher institution in a unified program. It will of necessity be employed, of course, in conjunction with the other methods which have been enumerated. But the actual substitution of a single program for the independent programs which are now carried on is the work of the agreement.

A single unified program has sometimes been assumed to mean the development of large concentration of facilities at some point or at several points in the area. This assumption has found support in trends to be observed among independent institutions and also in the action of the consolidation and the merger. Interchange of facilities under the agreement also implies concentration, since institutions must in most cases be located in proximity to each other in order to share offerings. The question may thus be raised whether a planned program for higher education will bring together in large groupings the facilities provided in the area. Dr. Ward, chairman of the Liberal Arts College Movement, protests:

> It may be good business sense for automobile manufacturers to concentrate their industries in a few cities, or in one city, like Detroit, for instance. It may be good business sense for department stores to concentrate in certain localities in the cities. But it would not be good business sense, certainly not good educational sense, to take 1,000,000 boys and girls, between the ages of 18 and 22, and try to educate them all in one place or in a few educational centers.[21]

Not only has concentration of facilities the disadvantages feared by Dr. Ward but when carried to extremes it removes higher educational opportunity from the local community. Many students as yet and probably for a considerable time in future will be unable to bear the expense of attending institutions located at a distance. It would seem, therefore, that any higher educational program for the area must plan on local provision where such appears to be needed.

The trend toward local provision is already to be observed on the part of many institutions. Most obvious has been the rapid rise

[21] "Future of the American College Provokes a Debate." *The New York Times,* December 31, 1931.

of the junior college. Another significant movement has been the development of extension services and the institution of extramural courses. In many cases universities have established branch institutions. Even in those states where unified control for all public institutions has been worked out, there have generally been maintained a number of separately located campuses to each of which is assigned a portion of the general undertaking. Colleges and universities appear to be realizing to an increasing degree their obligations to the large region in which they happen to be situated.

The assumption seems to be warranted, therefore, that local provision will play a very significant part in the planned program for the area. But this local provision should not be looked upon simply as the institution of elementary courses for the community. There seems reason to believe that such a point of view has been overemphasized as a result of the junior college movement. Probably extension courses have also emphasized to an extreme degree the fact that local provision must be general in character. As opposed to such belief is the concept that the local institution should be thoroughly adapted to the constituency which it serves. Thus, where possible the local institution should develop outstanding facilities in its field of emphasis. It should become a differentiated institution, providing advanced opportunities that are not offered elsewhere in the area and by this means affording high opportunity for its own students and also attracting other students specializing in its field or wishing to profit by its resources.

The movement toward the development of differentiated, local institutions is opposed to concentration and in its nature is a movement toward distribution. It may be worked out through the agency of branch institutions established under the control of a board of a larger institution located at a distance. It may be accomplished through the linking of institutions already in existence to others by agreement. Thus, the established college, by forming an agreement with a large university in a neighboring city, may develop along distinctive and unique lines.

Even now a trend seems to have set in against enormous student bodies. At Yale and Harvard the undergraduate groupings have been broken up into colleges and houses in each of which live two hundred fifty or three hundred students. At Columbia a residential college located a hundred miles away has been incorporated in the university system. This small college, Bard College, formerly St.

Stephen's College, is not alone another college which has become part of the university, but is rapidly becoming a distinctive college with unique offerings. The development of the area or regional plan for higher education will doubtless make possible elsewhere changes in this direction.

SUMMARY

This chapter has attempted to point out that cooperative planning involves coordination and that such planning is likely to occur for the present at least in the area rather than in the nation as a whole. There were discussed the various uses of the consolidation, the agreement, differentiation, restriction of offerings, and abandonment of institutions in cooperative planning of higher education. It was pointed out that all these methods might be employed either separately or in combination, but it was also pointed out that, because of the continuance of separately controlled institutions within an area, cooperative planning of higher education would seemingly have to depend upon the employment of the inter-institutional agreement. In various phases of the discussion the chapter attempted to emphasize the importance not only of adequate range of offerings for higher education but also of high quality provision. Finally, there were indicated briefly certain trends among higher institutions toward concentration of facilities at some central point or points and toward the extension of offerings in order to provide for all portions of the area.

CHAPTER X

General Summary and Conclusions

THIS investigation sought to solve seven problems: the extent to which agreements had been developed; the conditions governing the formation of agreements; the changes in institutional structure and function occurring under agreement; the type of safeguards set up by agreements for protecting institutional identity and powers; the values sought under agreement; the characteristics of undesirable agreements; and the implications of the agreement for cooperative planning of higher education.

Investigation of the first problem indicated that agreements had been formed in considerable numbers and that they were not limited to any particular type or kind of higher institution. It was shown that certain institutions had formed numerous agreements. Finally, it was shown that certain agreements were incompletely recorded and that the relationships established by agreements differed widely.

Study of the second problem showed that agreements were formed in almost all cases for the purpose of supplementing institutional offerings. Institutions whose programs in the main were dissimilar tended to form agreements. Thus the university and the professional school were the most fertile fields for the growth of agreements. Other factors, such as proximity and urban location, prospect of financial savings, institutional recognition, and service to the area, also play a part but the dominant factor would seem to be the opportunity to improve and increase the scope of institutional offering through supplementation of facilities.

Study of the third problem reinforced the belief that agreements are instituted primarily to facilitate interchange of offerings. It indicated that changes in structure varied widely and were developed according to patterns which had been worked out in most cases by individual institutions. It indicated also that the evaluation of different forms of structure is not possible on the basis of the material at hand for this study. As surveys of institutional resources and objectives bring into perspective more clearly the opportunities for agreements, evaluation of structure patterns will doubtless be possible to a greater degree.

The investigation of the fourth problem indicated the necessity for special provisions to clarify the relationship set up under agreement. It would seem that agreements must be based on an exact understanding at the outset of the obligations and privileges implied.

Study of the fifth problem showed that many values were sought under agreements. These, in general, fell into two groups: The first comprised advantages as to programs, their maintenance and improvement. The second comprised advantages as to preservation and augmentation of institutional distinctive character.

Study of the sixth problem, based as it was on the documents alone, could only indicate what would seem to be undesirable characteristics of agreements. Study of the agreements in operation would probably modify to greater or less degree the list of characteristics presented. Agreements seem to be undesirable where they perpetuate low quality offerings and duplication. They seem to be undesirable where they involve obligations to one of the contracting parties that have not been understood at the outset or that are not, in general, compensated for by benefits received.

Study of the seventh problem sought to indicate the function of the agreement and certain other methods of coordination in cooperative planning of higher education. It also sought to indicate the relationship of the agreement to these other methods. In the discussion there was emphasized the necessity for high quality offerings in all lines that the area sought to provide. There was also indicated the necessity for offerings of adequate scope and the implication that cooperative planning must make provision accessible to all portions of the area.

There follow certain conclusions which have grown out of this study. It is hoped that these will prove valuable to institutions concerning themselves with the inter-institutional agreement.

1. Agreements require, prior to their formation, a thorough investigation of institutional resources and objectives.

2. Agreements should be formed between institutions whose offerings are of high quality and recognized value.

3. Agreements should be employed to differentiate institutional programs and to limit institutional offerings to those services which the institutions can most adequately provide, and for which there is felt to be real need.

4. Agreements should be drawn up in writing and should describe as fully as possible the expected relationship to be established.

5. The terms of agreements should be recorded accurately and completely in order that they may act as guides for the relationship that is developed.

6. Agreements should specifically state which institution shall exercise authority in all cases where there is likely to be conflict of interests.

7. Agreements should provide for compensation of one institution by the other for services rendered.

8. Agreements should be formulated for the purpose of increasing and improving higher educational opportunities of the area in which the institutions are located.

9. More intensive study should be directed toward the evaluation of certain forms of structure for coordinating the work of higher institutions.

10. Neighboring institutions should undertake conferences for determining where agreements may be wisely employed and by what means cooperative planning may most effectively be carried on.